Visual Sources Series

THE INDUSTRIAL REVOLUTION 1750–1830

Peter Lane

Principal Lecturer in History,
Coloma College of Education, Kent

B. T. BATSFORD LTD   London

Uniform with this volume
THE VICTORIAN AGE
THE TWENTIETH CENTURY

First published 1972
© Peter Lane, 1972

ISBNO 7134 1720 X

Filmset by Keyspools Ltd, Golborne, Lancs.

Printed in Great Britain by Anchor Press, Tiptree, Essex
for the Publishers
B. T. Batsford Ltd, 4 Fitzhardinge Street, London W1

Contents

Acknowledgment

The author and the publishers wish to thank the following for permission to reproduce the illustrations in this book: The British Museum for Chapter 1, fig. 1, Chapter 2, fig. 5, Chapter 3, figs. 6, 7 and 10, Chapter 4, fig. 2, Chapter 5, figs. 2, 3 and 7, Chapter 6, figs. 2 and 3, Chapter 7, fig. 6; The Bodleian Library for Chapter 3, fig. 1; Carlisle Council for Chapter 6, fig. 6; City Art Gallery, Manchester for Chapter 1, fig. 3; City of Birmingham Corporation for Chapter 1, fig. 8; County Borough of Luton Museum and Art Gallery for Chapter 1, fig. 7; Courtauld Institute for Chapter 1, fig. 4; Cyfarthfa Castle Museum for Chapter 9, fig. 2; The Mansell Collection for Chapter 1, fig. 6; Chapter 2, figs. 5 and 7; Chapter 4, fig. 7, Chapter 6, figs. 7 and 8, Chapter 7, figs. 2, 4, 5, 7 and 8, Chapter 8, figs. 5 and 7, Chapter 9, figs. 5, 7 and 8, Chapter 10, figs. 2, 6 and 7, Chapter 11, figs. 3, 7 and 8; Museum of British Transport for Chapter 4, fig. 5; National Maritime Museum for Chapter 4, fig. 8; National Portrait Gallery for Chapter 6, fig. 1 and for the portraits of Raikes, Owen, Pitt, Wesley and Bentham; Newcastle-under-Lyme Museum for Chapter 6, fig. 5; Plymouth Public Libraries for Chapter 10, fig. 3; Radio Times Hulton Picture Library for Chapter 1, figs. 3, Chapter 3, fig. 2, Chapter 5, fig. 1, Chapter 10, fig. 5, Chapter 11, figs. 1, 4, 5 and 6, and for the portraits of Watt, Townshend, Telford, Wilkes, Jane Austen, Mary Godwin and Malthus; Science Museum, London, for Chapter 2, fig. 3; Tate Gallery for Chapter 9, fig. 6; University of Reading Museum of Rural Life for Chapter 3, figs. 3 and 5; Victoria and Albert Museum for Chapter 9, fig. 1 and Chapter 11, fig. 2; Josiah Wedgwood and Sons Ltd., for Chapter 1, fig. 5 and Chapter 4, fig. 4; The Wellcome Trustees for Chapter 5, figs. 4, 5 and 6.

The Illustrations

Introduction

How do we know what life was really like in the past? How do the writers of history books find out? Well, if they are writing about Ancient Times they may have to rely partly on a study of ruins (such as Stonehenge), of remains dug up by archaeologists (as at Sutton Hoo), of drawings made by cavemen or tools used by Bronze Age workmen. All of these things are 'documents' which tell us something about the past.

If the historian is writing about more modern times he can use written or printed material such as the diaries of Samuel Pepys or the Reports of Royal Commissions into factory conditions in the nineteenth century. Nowadays many of these printed documents have been published so that they can be used by young history students. We no longer have to rely completely on the text-book for our ideas of what life was like in 1500 or 1700 or 1900; we can now read the official documents ourselves.

Most of these collections of documents consist of printed material. This is almost natural since history is, after all, a story and a story is best told in words. But some of these printed documents are very long, the language is often very difficult, so that many of us are unwilling to use them.

It is different with illustrated material; we have an example of the difference if we look at the beginning of the 'Shelter' campaign. There had been dozens of Blue Books and White Papers on the problems of housing in modern Britain; there had been many learned articles, as well as shorter articles in the popular newspapers. But it was only after the BBC had shown the play *Cathy Come Home* that the real plight of the homeless was brought home to people; on the day after the first showing of this film, Des Wilson and a group of young friends decided to do something and 'Shelter' was born. The visual evidence had made much more impact on them than had the written word.

The same is true of the social history of modern Britain. We can, of course, study it through the written document, but we may understand the problem of nineteenth-century poverty much more clearly if we see a contemporary photograph of a group of barefooted children (Book 2, Chapter 9, Picture 8). Similarly, we can read about the problems of old age, but the photograph of the inmates of an Old People's Home in 1880 (Book 2, Chapter 7, Picture 6), brings out clearly what life was really like for these unfortunate people.

Of course the picture document, like the written document, has to be used very carefully by the historian. He has to ask questions about it, compare one picture with another, compare the evidence presented by the photograph with the evidence collected elsewhere – in the written word for example. It would be bad history, for instance, to conclude that all working-class people were very poor in 1900, yet this is certainly the evidence of some pictures (Book 2, Chapter 7, Pictures 7 and 10). But these pictures do not tell the whole story because there were other working-class people who were well off at this time (Book 2, Chapter 8, Picture 2). The job of the historian is to weigh up one piece of evidence with another before he begins to write his story.

In these three volumes I have tried to show how the historian works; there are questions about the pictures which will help to bring out the significance of the evidence presented; there are other questions which ask the Young Historian to compare one piece of evidence with another; there are questions which direct the Young Historian's attention to plays, novels or other written documents.

I have also tried to offer the Young Historian a variety of work – painting, letter-writing, reading – which will help him to recreate for himself, by his own imagination, what the past was like. These questions are not meant to be a final, complete list; there are many other questions to be asked on the pictures and many other kinds of work that might be tackled. The questions, like the picture-documents, are only illustrative and not exhaustive.

1 Living standards 1750–1830

My income and yours

In *David Copperfield*, Mr Micawber said: 'Annual income twenty pounds, annual expenditure nineteen pounds, nineteen and six – result happiness. Annual income twenty pounds, annual expenditure twenty pounds, ought and sixpence – result misery'. Each of us knows that Mr Micawber was right – we cannot spend more than we earn. Our personal income is one of the main factors which decides the standard at which we live – what kind of house, clothes, furniture and food we have, what holidays we enjoy, how we travel and spend our leisure time. If we have a small income we enjoy a lower standard of living than people who have a high income.

Our income is one factor which decides our living standards. Another factor is our own decision on how we spend that income. If we decide to save a good deal of our income then we will have a lower standard of living than if we had spent it all. Similarly, if we decide to spend a lot of money on clothes then we will have less to spend on holidays.

The nation's income

Every day the people of this country use their *labour* and, with the help of different kinds of machinery or equipment (or *capital*) they produce certain goods or provide certain services. In some cases this produce is easy to measure; we can go to a brickyard and count the number of bricks which the men have made in a day. In other cases it is difficult to measure accurately what a person has produced at the end of a day. How, for example, can we measure the output of a teacher or a nurse?

One way is to add up the incomes which people receive for the work they do – whether producing something like bricks or cars, or providing some service such as teachers, nurses, clerks and many others do. The total of their incomes is the *nation's income* – and is a measure of the goods and services provided by the nation.

Some nations have a high income – the USA in 1970 had an average income of about £800 per person (man, woman and child). In Britain the average is about £500. In India it is about £30. The main reason for the differences between these countries is the difference in their industrial development. America has gone further along the road of industrial progress; her workpeople produce more wealth each working hour than do the people of Britain – who in turn produce much more than do the people in India.

9

National income and living standards

The USA has a very high national income – and the people of the USA enjoy a very high standard of living. They have more cars, better roads, more university students, bigger newspapers and more varied food than the British have. Both the Americans and the British have more telephones, schoolteachers and holidays than the Indians can afford. As countries become more industrialised so the nation's income rises – and so does the standard of living of its inhabitants.

Dividing the nation's income

We have seen that the size of our personal income is only one factor in deciding our standard of living; another important factor is the decisions we make about the use of that income. In the same way the nation's total income is only one factor in deciding its standard of living; another important factor is the answer given to the question: 'How is the national income to be divided up?' There are many ways in which we might spend part or indeed all of the income; we might spend more on defence or war, or build more offices, hospitals and schools – and fewer houses, bridges and factories. We might spend more on food and less on machinery, more on entertainment and less on education.

Social history and the nation's income

In this volume we will see that the nation's income increased as a result of the first stages of the industrial revolution; we will also see the various ways in which this increased income was spent. In later volumes we will take the story up to our own time and notice both a continuing increase in the nation's income and the changes in the ways in which it was spent.

Britain in the middle eighteenth century

Britain in 1750 was a very different country from the one we know. The population was about five million; apart from London (with a population of about half a million), Bristol, Norwich, Exeter, Newcastle and Liverpool were the largest towns with populations of about 30,000 Manchester was described by Daniel Defoe as 'the largest mere village in England', with a population of about 10,000 in 1740.

Some of the people worked in industry (Chapter 2) but most were engaged in agriculture (Chapter 3), although most villagers earned money in the woollen industry, which was organised as a domestic industry. In Picture 2 you can see the interior of an eighteenth-century cottage. One writer noted: 'Every cottage has its wheel, every village its loom'. You will realise that the amount of material (and income) produced in this domestic system was small compared to that produced by each worker in the factory system (Picture 6).

Agricultural methods had changed little over the previous two or three centuries. As Picture 3 shows, both the plough and the method of ploughing was primitive. The hovel in the background was home for these workers and

1 Mining copper ore in Cornwall had provided work for people of all ages, and both sexes for centuries.

2 Cottage industry in pre-industrialised England – spinning. The old lady on the left is winding yarn into skeins for weaving.

3 Eighteenth century wheeled hoe being pulled by two men, with a hovel in the background.

4 The cottage lunch – from a somewhat idealised painting of country life by G. Morland.

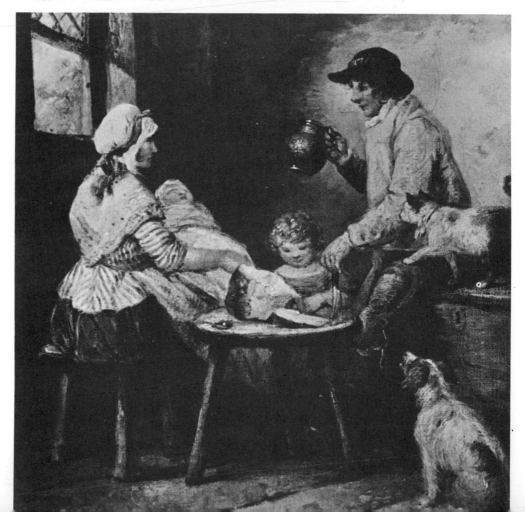

5 The Wedgwood family.

their families – and is a proof of their low income. George Morland's painting *The Cottage Lunch* (Picture 4) was meant to show how good life was in the village. If you look at the furniture, the food, the clothes, you will see that the standard-of-living of these people was low compared to that which we enjoy today – because they produced very little in the course of a day's work.

Some people were better off than this. There were the landed aristocrats who got most of their money from the rents paid by tenant farmers and lived in great houses (Chapter 5). There were middle-class families such as the Wedgwoods (Picture 5). The clothing, garden and general appearance of this pottery manufacturer's family show that their income was very high. Families such as these – the subjects of the novels by W. M. Thackeray and Jane Austen – could afford luxuries such as education, and could pay for such things as libraries (Picture 9). For the mass of the population, however, life was simple and often very hard.

Britain in 1830
By 1830 Britain had undergone the first stages of the industrial revolution; thousands of domestic workers had to abandon their spinning wheels and hand-looms and go to work in the factories springing up in the North, the Midlands and South Wales. The woollen industry was no longer the most important of Britain's industries; cotton had taken its place and the coal, iron and other industries were expanding rapidly (Chapter 2).

In Picture 6 you can see the interior of a Manchester mill with its huge, expensive machines which produced a hundred times more material per hour

6 A Manchester mill with machines for carding, drawing and rowing to prepare the cotton for spinning, 1843.

than was produced in the cottage system. The agricultural industry also underwent change; Picture 7 shows one of the new ploughs that were invented in this period, making the farmer more productive than he had been. This increased productivity of the farm worker and the industrial worker was the main reason for the increase in Britain's national income at this time.

Part of this income was spent on building new and better machines; part on building imposing churches and houses for the well-to-do. Some of it was spent on building new factories, some on the construction of canals. Very little, however, of this increased income was left for the building of houses for the working classes and little left over for them to spend on food, clothing or entertainment. Most of the British workers of the nineteenth century had to wait a long time

7 A plough – one of many machines invented during the eighteenth century to make agriculture more productive.

8 Birmingham. The development of factory-based industries led to the growth of such towns.

before they shared in the increasing prosperity of their country. As Dr J. P. Kay wrote in 1832:

> The population employed in the cotton factories rises at five o'clock, works from six till eight o'clock and returns home for half an hour to breakfast. This meal generally consists of tea or coffee with a little bread. Oatmeal porridge is sometimes, but of late, rarely used. The operatives return to the mills until twelve o'clock when an hour is allowed for dinner (which generally consists of boiled potatoes. The mess of potatoes is put into one large dish and a few pieces of fried fat bacon are sometimes mingled with them, but seldom meat. At the end of the hour they are all again employed in the mills, where they continue until seven o'clock or a later hour, when they generally again indulge in tea, often mingled with spirits, accompanied by a little bread.

9 A middle-class lending library in 1813.

1 The Young Historian

1   In Picture 1 you can see women at work. Can you say where the men may be working?

2   Name the different jobs being done in Picture 2. Find out the origin of the word 'spinster'.

3   Picture 4 is called *The Cottage Lunch*. What is the worker having for lunch? Can you say why this family could not afford better food or furniture?

4   There are children in both Pictures 4 and 5. Would you prefer to be the child in the cottage or in the Wedgwood family? Why?

5   Picture 9 shows the interior of a library in 1813. What sort of people are using the library? Why did the people from the cottage (Pictures 2 and 4) or from the copper mines (Picture 1) not go to such libraries?

6   In Picture 6 you can see children working in an early mill. Imagine that you are one of those children. Write a letter to your cousin in the cottage (Picture 2) telling him or her about life in the mill. (You might write about hours of work, the noise, amount of material produced.)

7   Picture 8 is a view of Birmingham. Find out what the main industries of this town were. What were the advantages and disadvantages of living in Birmingham compared with living in the hovel in Picture 3?

8   Why did the workers in the eighteenth-century industries (Picture 1) and farms (Pictures 2 and 3) need less education than workers in the nineteenth-century mills (Picture 6)? Can you say why the nineteenth century could afford to spend more money on schools and teachers than could the eighteenth century?

2 Industrial Changes

In Chapter 1 we saw that the main occupation of the British people in the eighteenth century was agriculture, although there was a thriving domestic woollen industry. There were a number of other industries including ship-building, pottery, steelmaking and brewing. Very few manufacturers imitated Thomas Lombe who at his mill employed 300 workmen. He was considered a 'large employer' in a country where most work was carried on in the cottage (Chapter 1, Picture 2). Mrs Gaskell, a nineteenth-century novelist, described the blissful life of the domestic weaver in 1800. She saw him as a man who,

> (with) all the processes carried on under his roof retained his individual respectability; he generally earned wages which enabled him to rent a few acres of land which filled up the vacant hours when he found it unnecessary to apply himself to his loom or spinning machine. (Men) of simple habits and few wants, the uses of tea, coffee and groceries but little known, they rarely left their own homestead. Grey-haired men have thus lived through a long life and have never entered a town. It is true that the quantity of cloth or yarn produced was but limited – for he worked by the rule of his strength and convenience. They were, however, sufficient to clothe and feed himself and his family decently, and according to their station.

1 Thorncliff ironworks 1810 – an early example of industrialisation, still in a rural setting.

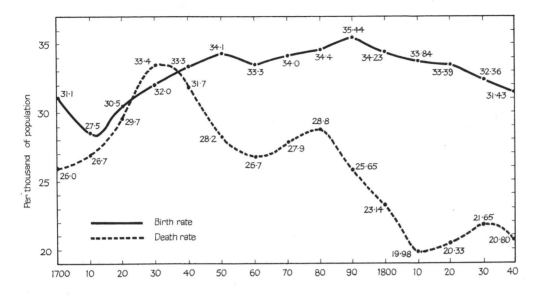

2 A graph showing population changes between 1700 and 1840.

One of the reasons why this slow, domestic system had to change can be seen in Picture 2 which shows that there was an almost continual fall in the death rate in the eighteenth century whilst there was a much slower fall in the birth rate in the same period. This increase in population had to be fed (so farming methods had to change); it also had to be clothed (so methods of production had to change in the textile industry). At the same time Britain acquired a large Empire – in India, Canada and the West Indies – which provided a large market for British goods, if only they could be produced in sufficient quantities. The domestic system obviously could not cope with these two increases in demand; change had to come.

There were many changes in the textile industry; a series of inventions by Kay, Hargreaves, Arkwright and Cartwright led to the production of huge, expensive machines driven first by water power and later by steam. Since these could not be housed in the workers' cottages, factories had to be built – at first, near quick-flowing streams, and later near coalfields where men, women and children worked at these new machines (Chapter 1, Picture 6; and Chapter 8, Picture 4).

Perhaps the most important invention of the period was the steam engine produced by James Watt in 1782. This was not the first steam engine; Thomas Savery in 1695 and Thomas Newcomen in 1712 had produced steam engines which were used to pump water out of coal and tin mines. Their engines, however, had only a pumping action – a to-and-fro action. Watt's invention was to use these engines in conjunction with his own idea of a gearing system so

3 Watt's rotative beam engine, 1788.

that the engines had a rotative action – and so could be used to drive machinery. This engine was quickly taken up by textile manufacturers and led to a rapid increase in the demand for coal, the fuel that drove these engines (Picture 4).

The iron age

There had been an iron industry in Britain for many centuries and iron foundries – employing a dozen or so men – were common in the Weald of Kent and Shropshire and other areas where the ironmasters could get a ready supply of charcoal. This was produced by burning some of the millions of trees in underpopulated but richly-forested areas of Britain. Several people had tried to use coal as a substitute for this expensive charcoal – the supply of the latter would one day have died out when all the trees were burned. However, they had always found that impurities from the coal got into the iron and ruined their product.

Fortunately Abraham Darby and his son, who had a works at Coalbrookdale

4   Working the ten-yard coal seam at Bradley Mine in Staffordshire.

(Picture 5) discovered how to get rid of the sulphur from the coal. They burned the coal and converted it into coke, which they found could be used to make good iron. This drove the ironmasters away from the forests and into the coalfields of the North, the Midlands, South Wales and the Scottish Lowlands. These new coke-operated furnaces made a pig iron (so called because the molten iron was poured from the furnaces into moulds which were called pigs). Pig iron was not as valuable or tough as wrought iron – made by re-smelting the pig iron with charcoal and hammering out the remaining impurities. In 1794 Henry Cort invented a reverberatory furnace in which the ore was heated and stirred to produce wrought iron fifteen times more quickly than before. He also invented grooved rollers which would change the large ingots of wrought iron into thinner, and more usable bars and sheets.

'Satanic Mills'
William Blake, the nineteenth-century poet, wrote of the Dark Satanic Mills

5 Ironworks at Coalbrookdale.

6 An early mill – power loom weaving.

of industrial Britain. Certainly they were dirty and dangerous but they were also productive places (Picture 6). Equally dirty and dangerous were the many new coal mines where women and children went to work before the sun rose, and from which they emerged after the sun had set (Picture 7). As Disraeli noted in his novel *Sybil*:

> They come forth; the mine delivers its gang and the pit its bondsmen; the forge is silent and the engine is still. The plain is covered with the swarming multitude; ... troops of youth – alas! of both sexes – though neither their raiment nor their language indicates the difference; all are clad in male attire; and oaths that men might shudder at issue from lips born to breathe words of sweetness. Yes, these are to be – some are – the mothers of England! But can we wonder at the hideous coarseness of their language when we remember the savage rudeness of their lives? Naked to the waist, an iron chain fastened to a belt of leather runs between their legs clad in canvas trousers, while on hands and feet an English girl, for twelve, sometimes sixteen hours a day, hauls and hurries tubs of coal up subterranean roads, dark and precipitous.

As British industry grew so there was a growing demand for coal, iron (Chapter 7, Picture 5) and textiles. More and more factories were built, around which there grew huge towns. Some of the towns were dedicated to spinning, others to weaving; some were commercial towns (such as Manchester), others were ports (such as Liverpool). But everywhere – in textile town and port, iron town and colliery village – the story was the same: a rapid increase in population.

7 Child labour in the mines, 1845.

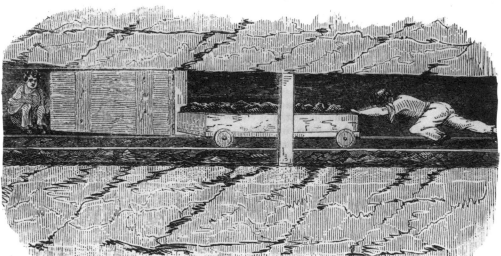

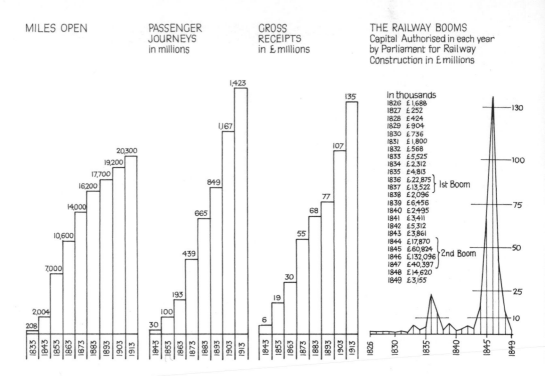

MILES OPEN
PASSENGER JOURNEYS in millions
GROSS RECEIPTS in £ millions
THE RAILWAY BOOMS
Capital Authorised in each year by Parliament for Railway Construction in £ millions

In thousands
1826 £ 1,688
1827 £ 252
1828 £ 424
1829 £ 904
1830 £ 736
1831 £ 1,800
1832 £ 568
1833 £5,525
1834 £2,312
1835 £4,813
1836 £22,875 } 1st Boom
1837 £13,522
1838 £2,096
1839 £6,456
1840 £2,495
1841 £3,411
1842 £5,312
1843 £3,861
1844 £17,870 } 2nd Boom
1845 £60,824
1846 £132,096
1847 £40,397
1848 £14,620
1849 £3,155

8 Graph showing the expenditure on railways in the nineteenth century.

Income and living standards

The nation's income increased as more coal, more iron and more textiles were produced in the more efficient factories, foundries and mines. Some of this increased wealth was taken by the industrialists themselves. They soon learned to live like their social superiors – the landed aristocrats – by building huge houses in spacious parks, where they lived a pleasant life (Chapter 5, Pictures 1, 2; Chapter 9, Pictures 2 and 3). They even built new schools for their sons (Chapter 10, Pictures 1 and 3). Above all, they spent money on new industrial development – building more and bigger factories, more and better methods of transport (Chapter 4). The workers gained little from this increased wealth.

2 The Young Historian

1 Find out the names of two inventions which affected (i) spinning and (ii) weaving. Which was the first power-driven textile machine?

2 Picture 2 shows changes in the birth rate and death rate from 1700 to 1840. Was the population greater or smaller at the end of this period? Was this change due mainly to changes in the birth rate or changes in the death rate? Find out why this change took place.

24

3   Picture 3 shows one of the engines built by James Watt. Find out (i) whose engine Watt first worked on and improved, (ii) how his engine built in 1781 was different to previous engines.

4   Picture 5 shows the iron works at Coalbrookdale where the Darby family first smelted iron with coal. How had iron been smelted before this? Why did the use of coke and coal lead to a decline in the iron industries of Kent, and a growth of towns in South Wales and the North East of England?

5   Picture 7 shows a child at work in a coal mine. Imagine that you were this child, telling your country cousins (Chapter 1, Pictures 2 and 4) about a day's work.

6   Paint your own picture of either working in a mine or the interior of a cotton mill. You might make this part of a frieze to which you can add illustrations from later sections of this book.

7   Look again at Chapter 1, Picture 2, and now at Picture 6 in this Chapter. Can you suggest why Britain was a richer country in 1850 than in 1750? How was some of this increased wealth spent?

8   Picture 8 shows the amount of money spent on the building of railways between 1826 and 1849. Can you name three materials which had to be bought with this money, and three industries which expanded very rapidly because of this?

3 Agricultural Changes

The Strip System

We have seen in Chapter 1 that Britain was a country in which the greater part of the population lived in small towns or villages. Their main occupation was agriculture in which they used poor tools (Chapter 1, Picture 3) and produced very little, so that the standard of living was low (Chapter 1, Picture 4). In some parts of the country large farms had been created in the Tudor period so that sheep farming could be made profitable; but in many parts of the country the medieval three-field, strip system was practised. As the map shows (Picture 5), the fields (or furlongs) around the village were divided into strips, each villager being allocated a strip in each of the fields. You can see the different numbers along the strips. This method was very inefficient; time was wasted in going from one strip to another; land was wasted since there had to be a baulk (or small unploughed section) left between each strip. There was no protection for an efficient farmer from the weeds which might grow on his less efficient neighbour's land; there was no way of preventing animals wandering from place to place across strips, eating as they went.

The system had not changed for many centuries, and while the demand for food was limited by the size of the population (and of the town population in particular), the local farmer produced enough for his own needs and those of a known locality, which he served with the primitive methods of transport then available. The Yorkshire milk boys on their rounds sold what milk their master had got (Picture 1); there were no milk trains to carry the milk to London from Yorkshire.

1 Yorkshire milk boys

2 New agricultural machinery in the eighteenth-century – Jethro Tull's Wheat drill.

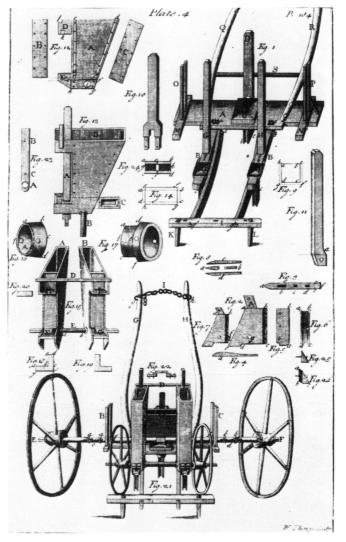

Eighteenth-century Changes

As we have seen (Chapter 2, Picture 2), the population increased in the eighteenth century and one result of this was an increased demand for food. This demand was cumulative, in that the domestic workers were beginning to leave their villages – and farming   for the towns where they could not produce their own food, and thus put further pressures upon the remaining farmers.

One way of making the farmer more efficient was to give him better equipment with which to work. A series of inventions beginning with Tull's seed drill (Picture 2), and including ploughs, reapers, and threshing machines, meant that the farm worker could produce more in a given time than his forefathers

3 Robert Bakewell at a ram letting.

with their primitive methods (Chapter 1, Picture 3). Although some tasks – such as haymaking – remained unmechanised throughout the nineteenth century and although many farmers did not use the more modern methods (Picture 4), many farm workers found that they were being replaced by machinery. Some went into the towns and joined the ranks of the industrial workers; others tried to stop the march of progress and, led by a Captain Swing,

4 Threshing and sowing from a book published in 1805.

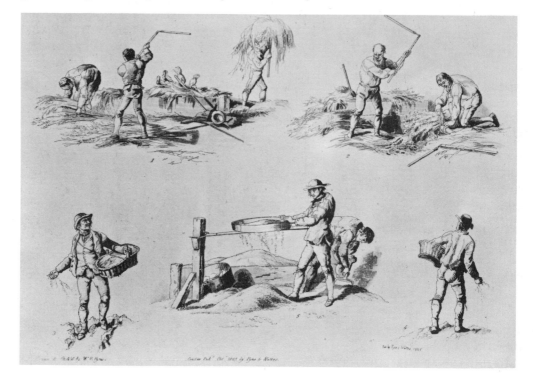

they rioted in the 1830s as the handbills make clear (Pictures 7 and 8). In the 1830s William Cobbett, the journalist, wrote:

> All across the South, from Kent to Cornwall, and from Sussex to Lincoln-shire, the commotion extended. It began by the labourers in Kent entering the buildings of the great farmers and breaking their threshing machines; . . . the labourers saw, at any rate, that the threshing machines robbed them of their wages. This was a crime; the magistrates were ready with punishments; soldiers were ready to shoot down the offenders. Unable to resist these united forces, the labourers resorted to the use of fire, secretly put to the barns and stacks of those who had the machines. They went in bands of from 100 to 1,000 and summoned the farmers to come forth, and then they demanded that they should agree to pay them such wages as they thought right. The military force backed by all the great farmers, the landowners, and especially the parsons, would have subdued these half-starved machine-breakers; but the Fires! No power on earth could have prevented them, if the millions of labourers resolved to resort to them.

Another way of making the land more productive was learned from the Dutch who had reclaimed much of their land from the sea and had been forced to discover how to make salty, sandy soil productive. English farmers, particularly those in the low-lying Fenlands, learned from them; they introduced the practice of marling in which lime and clay is added to sandy soil to make it richer; they brought in a number of root crops – turnips, swedes, mangels, as well as new types of grass, all of which helped to enrich the soil. These root crops also provided a new food for the people as well as a winter fodder for the cattle, horses and sheep. These new practices were first adopted by richer farmers (Picture 10) who had the money to spend on machinery as well as the education required to understand the importance of the more scientific Dutch methods.

Enclosure and Enclosure Acts

Land drainage and stockbreeding were costly undertakings and we have seen, too, that the introduction of new crops and methods was impossible in the strip system. If the new ideas were to be taken up, strips would have to be re-allocated so that each farmer had a compact or 'consolidated' farm which he could 'enclose'.

Between 1760 and 1793, 1,355 Enclosure Acts were passed: from 1793 to 1815 there were 1,934 Enclosure Acts and by 1850 nearly all the land in the country was enclosed. Sometimes, however, enclosure was done by agreement between all the owners concerned without any Act of Parliament being involved.

When the leading landowners of a parish wanted to petition Parliament for an Enclosure Act they had to fix a notice to the church door for three Sundays; they then drew up a Bill giving details of their scheme, which was examined by a Committee of the House of Commons. The owners of three-quarters of the

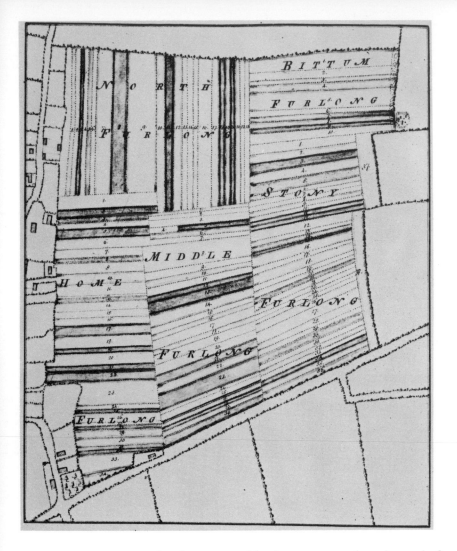

5 Map of a strip farmed village.

land concerned had to agree to the scheme before it could be presented; objectors could present evidence before the House of Commons while the scheme was being examined there. If the Bill was passed through the House of Commons, three Commissioners were appointed to carry out the enclosure.

The Commissioners mapped out the land, checked everyone's claim to a share, divided the land and settled all disputes concerning fencing, pasture rights, ownership of woods, and so on. Enclosure caused hardship to many people, who lost their land as a result of it, and riots were common. As the House of Commons *Journal* noted in 1814:

> It was impracticable to affix the Notices (of enclosures) on the Church doors (of Otmoor) owing to large mobs, armed with every description of offensive weapons, having assembled for the purpose of obstructing the persons who went to affix the notices, and who were prevented by violence, and threats of immediate death, from approaching the Churches.

In 1793 the Government had appointed Arthur Young to head the Board of

Agriculture and Young, who had written so persuasively in favour of the new methods and had travelled widely throughout England, studying these methods and telling others about them, could now help to organise the formation of local Agricultural Societies and Shows where the less progressive farmer could learn about the methods of his more enterprising brethren.

Stock-breeding

Before the coming of the root vegetable most British animals were killed off in autumn and the meat salted down for use in the winter, or they were left to fend for themselves throughout the winter, eating 'what God Almighty provided'. The result was that British cattle, sheep and horses were generally of a poor quality. Robert Bakewell made a study of the problems of stock-breeding, experimented on his own animals and proved thst selective breeding of the best males with the best female animals could improve the quality of a breed; the animals were heavier, they produced more milk, wool and meat. He was helped in his work by the improved quality of winter food available; he was also imitated by a number of other rich farmers such as the Duke of Bedford, the Collings Brothers, and Thomas Coke of Holkham. Such men hired out their animals to neighbouring farmers so that their stock could be improved; Bakewell, seen in Picture 3 at a ram letting, earned £1,200 a year from hiring out three of his rams.

Agricultural Living Standards

The enclosure movement had its good side – there was more and better food of different varieties available for the increasing town populations. The movement also had its bad side as it meant the end of the small strip farmer who had provided for himself and his family while his wife and children earned extra money in the domestic system. Many leaseholders and copyholders were driven from the land; many freeholders were unable to compete with the more efficient and larger farmer. The large farmer, sometimes a landed aristocrat, often a tenant of some noble lord, had great political influence in the unreformed and corrupt Parliamentary system of the period (Chapter 6, Pictures 2 and 4). When the price of British food rose during the Napoleonic wars these farmers prospered; when this prosperity was threatened by the promise of the import of foreign (cheaper) food at the end of the war, they used their influence to force Parliament to pass the Corn Laws which kept the price of bread very high.

At the same time wages in the towns were low and unemployment common, and life was very hard for the ordinary people. Sometimes they demanded a change in a system which favoured only the few (Picture 7); meetings such as the one at Peterloo (Chapter 6, Picture 8), were common; riots (Chapter 7, Pictures 7 and 8) were frequent and bloody. But in spite of these and the activities of Captain Swing, the landed gentry and their tenant farmers maintained their hold on Parliament throughout this period.

31

6 *Opposite, above.* One of many contemporary cartoons on the Napoleonic Wars – this one celebrates the convention of Cintra during the Peninsula War.

7 *Opposite, below.* Cartoon on the parliamentary system by which England was governed in 1831 by Cruikshank.

PUBLIC
NOTICE.

THE *Magistrates* in the Hundreds of *Tunstead* and *Happing*, in the County of Norfolk, having taken into consideration the disturbed state of the said Hundreds and the Country in general, wish to make it publicly known that *it is their opinion* that such disturbances principally arise from the use of Threshing Machines, and to the insufficient Wages of the Labourers. The Magistrates therefore beg to *recommend* to the Owners and Occupiers of Land in these Hundreds, to *discontinue the use of Threshing Machines, and to increase the Wages of Labour* to Ten Shillings a week for able bodied men, and that when task work is preferred, that it should be put out at such a rate as to enable an industrious man to earn Two Shillings per day.

The Magistrates are determined to enforce the Laws against all tumultuous Rioters and Incendiaries, and they look for support to all the respectable and well disposed part of the Community; at the same time they feel a full Conviction, that *no severe measures will be necessary*, if the proprietors of Land will give proper employment to the Poor on their own Occupations, and encourage their Tenants to do the same.

SIGNED,

JOHN WODEHOUSE.
W. R. ROUS.
J. PETRE.
GEORGE CUBITT.
WILLIAM GUNN.
W. F. WILKINSON.
BENJAMIN CUBITT.
H. ATKINSON.

North Walsham,
24th November 1830.

J. PLUMBLY, PRINTER, NORTH WALSHAM.

Notice issued by Norfolk magistrates, November 1830

this is to inform you what you have to undergo Jentelmen if providing you Dont pull down your neshines and rise the poor mens wages the maried men give tow and six pence a day a day the singel tow eshilings. or we will burn down your barns and you in them this is the last notis

from W Sh

8 'Captain Swing' notice.

9 A 'Captain Swing' letter from agricultural rioters explaining their case.

10 Satirical view of a rich farmer's household.

An increasing income from the land went to a few – the owners of the land and the farmers. As can be seen in Picture 10 such farmers had a high standard of living; so, too, did their landowning superiors (Chapter 5, Picture 1). Not so the ordinary people – their housing (Chapter 7, Picture 2), and furniture (Chapter 7, Picture 3), were very poor, as was their food (Chapter 7, Picture 6). The Rev. Daniel Davies was Rector of Barkham, and he noted in 1797:

> Many working men break-fast and dine on dry bread alone; their meal is supper, and that no better than unpeeled potatoes and salt and water. Clothes they get as they can, and the children go nearly naked.

3 The Young Historian

1   Picture 1 shows the milk boy on his round. Why could the Yorkshire farmer not sell his milk in London until after 1830? Write your own story of 'A day in the life of the milk boy'.

2   Look again at Picture 3 in Chapter 1 and now at Picture 2 in this chapter. Can you suggest why the supply of food increased? How did this affect the health of the people? (You should also look again at Picture 2 in Chapter 2, on population changes.)

3   Picture 3 shows Robert Bakewell hiring out his rams to other farmers so that their livestock could be improved. How was Bakewell's stock breeding helped by other farmers

growing turnips? Bakewell's work led to bigger sheep and cattle. How did this affect the lives of the British people? (Look again at Picture 2 in Chapter 2.)

4 Look at Picture 5. Imagine you had Strip 1 in each furlong (or field). Write your own criticism of this system of farming. (You might write about time, your neighbours on Strips 2 and 3, wandering animals.)

5 Pictures 8 and 9 are typical of hundreds of posters put up in England in the late 1820s and early 1830s. Can you list the reasons which drove many workers to riot and arson?

6 Find out the meaning of the words (i) freeholder, (ii) copyholder, (iii) leaseholder. Which of these suffered most when land was enclosed?

7 Look at Picture 4 in Chapter 1 again. Why was the price of bread so important to ordinary people? Find out why Parliament passed the Corn Laws in 1815.

8 Look at Picture 10 and Picture 7. Why was the rich farmer against any change in the Parliamentary system?

4 Transport Changes

The best roads in eighteenth-century Britain were those that had been built by the Romans while they occupied these islands after 55 BC. Most roads were mere tracks which became pitted and muddy during the rainy season, and dusty in the dry weather. The opening chapter of Dickens' *Tale of Two Cities* tells of the problems of the stage coach going from London to Dover; passengers had to get out and walk when the coach came to a hill. Newspaper accounts of this period tell us of the Exeter coach that was lost – and never found – on a journey through the snow to London.

Industry and Transport

If the increasing amount of food, building material, coal, iron, cotton and other goods were to be carried to and from Britain's growing industrial towns, then there would have to be an improvement in the method of transport. Some people realised this and formed turnpike trusts which were companies of local rich people, formed by an Act of Parliament, which gave them the duty of building and maintaining a stretch of road; in return for this they could erect toll gates and charge people who used that stretch of road (Picture 2). Turnpike trusts employed engineers such as Macadam, Metcalfe, Rennie and Telford to build their roads and they in turn engaged roadmakers to do the hard work (Picture 1). Their work was valuable but was limited to a few miles of main road leading into important towns. It was also limited by the quality of the materials and machinery available to their employees. However, although travelling by road remained a dangerous and difficult business throughout this period, their

1   Eighteenth century roadmakers.

2 Stage coach – the London to Exeter mail.

efforts did encourage the development of new, quicker stage coaches (Picture 2), by means of which richer people could travel or the mails could be carried. In 1813 General Dyott wrote:

> I found a very good stage coach that left Bath at eight am, and was two days on the road (to London).

In 1827 he wrote:

> ... travelling must have arrived at perfection. We travelled ninety-nine miles in twelve hours.

Certainly travel had improved since 1736 when Lord Hervey, living in Kensington, wrote:

> The road to London is so bad that we live here in the same solitude as if cast on a rock in the middle of the ocean.

The Canals

However, for ordinary people, there was little chance of their going by such coaches. Nor were the coaches of much use for the industrialist who wanted to carry huge quantities of bulky materials to his factory. For many centuries the British had used their rivers as a means of carrying heavy goods; the safest, though not shortest, journey from Chester to Shropshire was by sea – around Wales and then up the River Severn. In the eighteenth century many people saw the advantage of carrying their goods by water, and a number of them built their own canals. The most famous canal owner – because he is often thought of as the first – was the Duke of Bridgwater, who owned coal mines at Worsley and cotton mills ten miles away in Manchester. He wanted a cheap and quick method of getting the coal to the steam engines in his mills. He invited

3 Canal transport – a view of Barton bridge.

James Brindley to design and supervise the building of a canal (Picture 3). This involved the construction of aqueducts to carry the canal across rivers and valleys as well as a system of locks to help take the water up hillsides; it also meant the digging – by manual labour – of the huge canal ditch itself. Brindley succeeded; the canal earned a fortune for the Duke as well as leading to a fall in the price of coal in Manchester. Other people were encouraged to build canals and, by 1830, as Picture 9 shows, Britain was covered by a network of canals. As Picture 4 reveals, certain industrialists gained a great deal from this system; Josiah Wedgwood, for instance, needed masses of heavy clay for use in his potteries and then required a fast method of transporting his fragile products to their market. He built his own canal for this purpose.

British industrial towns could now be built rapidly since the building materials could be carried cheaply and speedily; factories could get raw materials and coal more easily, and could sell their finished products. Families could get food from the now distant countryside.

4 *Opposite*. Canal notice – an account of what Henshall & Co. carried for Wedgwoods in 1806.

Messrs Wedgwood & Co

The Company
Consider themselves entitled
to detain Goods for
Freight in Arrear.

To Hugh Henshall & Co.ᵈ Dᵣ

1806	For Freight	(Weight)				Burden			Rate	Amount		
		T	C	Q	lb	L	S	D		L	S	D
Mar 13	To Bill delivered —									221	16	10
22	9 Crates L.pool a Etruᵃ					"	3	"		"	3	"
	Clay R.K. & Jones	14	17	"	"	4	11	12/-		9	3	2
29	3 Crates Etruᵃ a Tipfifey		12	"	"						9	"
	8 Empty Casks Stourᵗ	"	"	"	"	3	4	6		3	12	6
	10 Empty Hhds Park	"	"	"	"	1	18	8		2	8	8
April 5	4 do Crates L.pool Dᵒ	"	"	"	"	"	3	8		"	3	8
	10 do Hhds Stourᵗ Dᵒ									"	10	
	Clay L.pool & Jon	14	9	"	"	"	4	10	12/-	8	18	3
	2 Casks Lead Preston	1	16	1	2	"	15	8	7/5	1	7	3
	1 Crate Etruᵃ	"	4	"	"					"	3	7
12	Chirtstone Leek Etruᵃ	6	10	"	"				3/9	1	4	5
	Clay L.pool Fayl	14	2	"	"	4	8		12/-	8	13	11
	1 Empty Crate						4			"	"	4
19	1 Hhd. 1 Tierce Etruᵃ G.H.H									"	14	—
	1 do 1 do O.L.L									"	4	"
	24 Empty Crates L.pool Etruᵃ									"	8	"
	1 Punᵗ Spirits	9	"	"				19/10		"	8	11
	1 Crate Etruᵃ	4	"	"						"	3	7
	1 Hhd, 1 Tierce U.W	14	"	"						"	12	7
	1 Box O.W	"	"	2	27					"	1	"
May 3	Clay L.pool Etruᵃ	8	7	"	"	2	9	12/-		5	3	"
	" Dᵒ	16	10	"	"	5	6	"		10	3	6
	" Dᵒ	15	10	"	"	5	2	"		9	11	2
	1 Crate 1 Box Etruᵃ		4	2	10					"	4	7
	Clay L.pool	16	2	"	"	5	4	12/-		9	18	7
	2 Crates Etruᵃ									"	7	2
17	1 Hhd Ware L.pool Noke	"	"	"	"	"	"	"		"	"	"
	28 Casks Clay Etruᵃ	32	"	"	"	4	6			19	8	6
	33 do "	8	5	"	"	1	"	"		5	"	"
	90 do "	22	10	"	"					13	10	
	2 Bags Potatoes Wine	3	2	20				6/5		1	3	
										335	4	5

5 Horse drawn train. Such trains, with wooden rails, were in common use near coal mines.

Early railways

A horse can pull a heavier weight in a barge than it could in a road wagon. Similarly, it can pull more on rails than along an ordinary road. For this reason there had been railways for many years – usually near coal mines where horse-drawn wagons were pulled along either wooden or iron rails (Picture 5). In 1804 Richard Trevithick had experimented with one of Watt's engines to produce a railway engine to pull wagons at the coal mine at Penydarren in South Wales; the experiment was only partially successful – the weight of the engine crushed the rails. But a mining engineer, George Stephenson, and his brother, Robert, carried on similar experiments in the North-East and in 1825 they built the first effective railway engine. They supervised the construction

6 An omnibus of 1829.

of a railway line linking Stockton and Darlington and in 1825 this line was opened – the first railway system on which passengers as well as goods were carried.

Experiments such as these and the construction of both canals and railways

7 The opening of the first English railway between Stockton and Darlington in 1825.

were only possible in a country which was already economically developing. A really poor country would not have had the skilled men needed – for designing and building – nor would it have had the materials they required – the steam engines, the iron rails and so on. Only a rich country could afford to use part of its income to improve its transport system; a poor country uses its income merely to survive. The new systems of canals and railways brought about an even faster economic development so that the nation's income increased as a result. It is for this reason that some people believe we should use 1830 as the beginning of a second stage in the industrial revolution. For once Britain had begun to build railways her wealth increased at such an enormous rate that in the next fifty years the country was transformed. Any Rip Van Winkle returning

8 Sailing ships – unloading a collier brig.

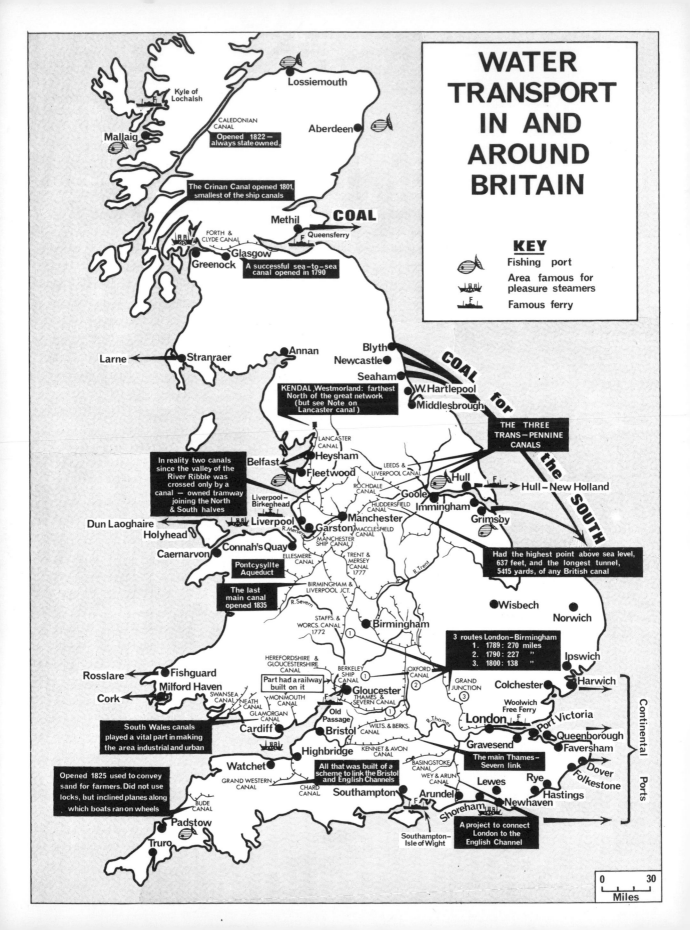

WATER TRANSPORT IN AND AROUND BRITAIN

KEY

Fishing port

Area famous for pleasure steamers

Famous ferry

Lossiemouth

Kyle of Lochalsh

Mallaig

Aberdeen

CALEDONIAN CANAL
Opened 1822 — always state owned.

The Crinan Canal opened 1801, smallest of the ship canals

Methil

COAL

FORTH & CLYDE CANAL

Queensferry

Glasgow

Greenock

A successful sea-to-sea canal opened in 1790

Larne

Stranraer

Annan

Blyth

Newcastle

Seaham

W. Hartlepool

Middlesbrough

KENDAL, Westmorland: farthest North of the great network (but see Note on Lancaster canal)

COAL for the SOUTH

THE THREE TRANS—PENNINE CANALS

LANCASTER CANAL

In reality two canals since the valley of the River Ribble was crossed only by a canal — owned tramway joining the North & South halves

Belfast

Heysham

Fleetwood

LEEDS & LIVERPOOL CANAL

Hull

Hull – New Holland

ROCHDALE CANAL

HUDDERSFIELD CANAL

Goole

Immingham

Liverpool-Birkenhead

Dun Laoghaire

Holyhead

Liverpool

R. Mersey

Garston

Manchester

MANCHESTER SHIP CANAL

MACCLESFIELD CANAL

Grimsby

Caernarvon

Connah's Quay

ELLESMERE CANAL

TRENT & MERSEY CANAL 1777

R. Trent

Had the highest point above sea level, 637 feet, and the longest tunnel, 5415 yards, of any British canal

Pontcysyllte Aqueduct

BIRMINGHAM & LIVERPOOL JCT.

The last main canal opened 1835

R. Severn

Wisbech

Norwich

STAFFS. & WORCS. CANAL 1772

Birmingham

3 routes London–Birmingham
1. 1789: 270 miles
2. 1790: 227 "
3. 1800: 138 "

Rosslare

Fishguard

Milford Haven

Cork

HEREFORDSHIRE & GLOUCESTERSHIRE CANAL

BERKELEY SHIP CANAL

OXFORD CANAL

Ipswich

GRAND JUNCTION

Colchester

Harwich

SWANSEA CANAL

NEATH CANAL

MONMOUTH CANAL

GLAMORGAN CANAL

Part had a railway built on it

Gloucester

THAMES & SEVERN CANAL

Woolwich Free Ferry

Port Victoria

South Wales canals played a vital part in making the area industrial and urban

Cardiff

Old Passage

Bristol

WILTS. & BERKS. CANAL

R. Thames

London

Queenborough

Gravesend

Faversham

Highbridge

KENNET & AVON CANAL

The main Thames – Severn link

Opened 1825 used to convey sand for farmers. Did not use locks, but inclined planes along which boats ran on wheels

Watchet

GRAND WESTERN CANAL

CHARD CANAL

All that was built of a scheme to link the Bristol and English Channels

BASINGSTOKE CANAL

WEY & ARUN CANAL

Lewes

Rye

Hastings

Dover

Folkestone

Southampton

Arundel

Shoreham

Newhaven

BUDE CANAL

Padstow

Truro

Southampton-Isle of Wight

A project to connect London to the English Channel

Continental Ports

0   30
Miles

in 1880 after a century's absence would have been utterly bewildered by the scope of the changes that had taken place.

Britain's industrial revolution was in part the result of overseas demand for more British goods. British exports to her colonies and to Europe grew throughout this period – in spite of the long Napoleonic Wars (Chapter 3, Picture 6), which in many ways served only to help British industry to develop. This foreign trade depended on the sailing ship – although a wooden steamship was already at work in the Firth of Clyde in 1809. The wooden sailing vessel carried Britain's goods abroad and brought back the increasing quantities of raw materials.

These ships were often built in America, where a plentiful supply of cheap timber and the need for ships to carry America's goods along her long seaboard had combined to produce a large number of very efficient shipbuilding yards. Britain's role as a leading shipbuilding nation did not begin until the steel ship had replaced the wooden one, and until steam engines had replaced sail. This did not happen until the next period of our study (1830–1914).

4 The Young Historian

1 Look at Pictures 1 and 2. Why did most roads become pitted and dangerous? How did this affect the transport of (i) heavy materials such as coal or clay and (ii) fragile articles such as china or pottery?

2 Find out why one horse can pull a heavier weight on a canal barge than six horses can pull in a wagon on the road.

3 Can you suggest some of the difficulties that faced the first canal builders? You might find it useful to investigate the meanings of aqueduct, lock-gates, puddling the bottom.

4 Look at Picture 4. What was the heaviest material carried? Why did Wedgwood need this material?

5 Why was the building of a canal system essential for (i) the building of the new industrial towns, (ii) supplying the new factories with fuel and raw material?

6 Write a letter describing your first trip on a stage coach.

7 Look at Picture 3. How are the barges being drawn across the aqueduct? Why? Can you suggest other methods of power that might have been used?

8 Look at Picture 6. Why were there traffic jams in the early industrial towns?

9 *Opposite.* Map of the canal system in Britain, 1760–1830.

5 Towns, Health and Housing

Until the middle of the eighteenth century the majority of the British people lived in small villages; Bristol and Norwich were the two largest towns outside London – and their population in 1750 was about 30,000. With the introduction of machinery in the 1770s and the increased demand for coal and iron, there was a growth of towns around the mines, the mills and the foundries. Following the expansion of foreign trade there was a similar growth of some ports, notably Liverpool. All these towns grew very rapidly: so that by 1830 there were many towns with populations of over 100,000, and very many with populations of over 50,000.

Local government

When a mine owner or mill owner decided to develop his business, houses had to be built for the workers. There was no national law laying down standards of housing, or the width of streets, nor had the builders of the new towns any experience in dealing with the problems of refuse disposal, sanitation or supplying 100,000 people with an adequate water supply. Nor were there strong local councils which might have made their own regulations about these matters. As we shall see (Chapter 9) there were only 178 local councils in 1750 and most of these existed in the older, agricultural parts of the country. There was no one to advise or restrain the people who built the mining towns of South Wales and the North East, or the spinning and weaving towns of Lancashire: there was a Lord of the Manor of Mosley who was responsible for the area in which the town of Manchester grew at this time – but he had neither the staff, experience nor ability to deal with the problems of the rapid growth of the new giant.

National income and housing

We have already seen that the nation has a certain amount of wealth out of which it has to provide its factories, shops, houses, reservoirs and everything else that it needs. In this period (1750–1830), as in any other period, there was an almost endless number of things that people would have liked to have done with their annual incomes; but in this period, as in any other, the annual income was not great enough to allow the nation to do everything. A choice had (and still has) to be made as to how this national income was to be spent. Since, as we have seen, there was a great deal of building of factories, new machinery, canals, bridges, early railways, and so on, there was only a limited amount of wealth left each year for the building of houses and the development of the new town.

1 Wentworth Wood House in Yorkshire.

In this situation the rich claimed some of the limited amount for their own houses: they either built new ones (Picture 2) or rebuilt older houses (Picture 1), very often under the influence of one or other of the great architects who were then building Regent Street, and Brighton and Bath as model towns for richer people. The less well-off had to be content with what was left. They had low wages and so could afford only a very low rent. The house owner or builder, knowing that he could expect only a low rent, provided only a low quality house. He tried to build as many houses on each acre as he could, and as near the factory or mine as he could – until there was a cheap method of transport late in the

2 A model villa.

3 Working class housing – Jacob's Island in London.

nineteenth century, workpeople had either to live near their place of work or walk a long distance. This meant that in Stockton, for example:

> Shepherd's Buildings consist of two rows of houses with a street seven yards wide between them: each row consists of . . . houses placed back to back; each house contains two rooms, viz. a house place and a sleeping room above: each room is about three yards wide and four long. . . . . In many of these dwellings there are four persons in one bed.

The individual house builder never felt it necessary to provide these working-class houses with either a water supply or a sanitary system. To have done so would have put up the price of the house and of the rent and might have increased the overcrowding as the number of families per house was increased. In some cases a builder constructed one toilet at the end of a row of, perhaps, 200 houses; nearby, he might put a stand pipe (Picture 4) from which the people would draw their water supply. In others, the builder constructed a common cess pit near the houses and as this often overflowed the houses were flooded with the sewage. Some towns took their water supply straight from rivers: Londoners took most of theirs from the Thames which was also the river into which they poured their sewage (Picture 7).

There was no provision for the construction of paved streets: streets were, for the most part, the muddy mess which you can see today on an unfinished housing estate. On to such streets was thrown the house refuse (since there was no system of refuse collection), so that these muddy thoroughfares became another potential source of disease as refuse rotted: there was never any organised street cleaning.

Poor water supplies, insufficient sanitation and disease-ridden streets, were common in the new industrial towns. Not surprisingly the death rate was very high as disease flourished (Picture 8). In 1842 over 350 out of every 1,000 babies died before reaching the age of one; the average life of a child born to working-class parents was only seventeen years, and even a child born to middle-class parents could expect to live only three years longer. These deaths were not due to accidents in factories (where middle-class children never worked): they were due to the insanitary conditions of the industrial and commercial towns. In the parish of St Martin-in-the-Fields, London, the vicar wrote:

> Some houses have from 45 to 60 persons of all ages under one roof, and in the event of death, the body often occupies the only bed till they raise money to pay for a coffin, which is often several days. .... Of course the tenants are never free from fevers and diarrhoea and the mortality is great. ... I have known six people sleep in a room about nine feet square, with only one small window, about 17 inches by 12 inches.

4 A stand-pipe in Clerkenwell (1863). The one pipe served many houses and the water was only turned on for twenty minutes a day.

Local action

Occasionally public-spirited inhabitants would group together and pay for the passage of a Private Act of Parliament so that their town would have the right to appoint Improvement Commissioners who would be responsible for enforcing rules about house building, or street cleansing or refuse disposal. But such Acts were very expensive to push through Parliament, and even after they were passed people resented the interference by Commissioners or their clerks with the freedom of builders and factory owners to do as they wished. In addition, by the time the Commissioners had been appointed to deal with a particular problem in a particular town, very often that town had grown even larger and new problems had been created for which they had no powers. Until strong local authorities were created in Victorian England, and until Parliament passed laws about housing and sanitary conditions, there was very little improvement in amenities in the industrial towns.

Disease flourished in towns and villages due, largely, to insanitary conditions. Another reason for the high death rate was the state of medical knowledge. In the later eighteenth century Edward Jenner had discovered a cure for smallpox

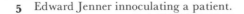

5 Edward Jenner innoculating a patient.

6 Dr James Lind.

7 Pollution of the Thames at Southwark Water Works.

(Picture 5): until late in the nineteenth century no one knew how cholera, diptheria and other diseases originated; thus no one could even begin to try to discover a cure for these. A poorly-paid, badly-housed people could afford only a poor diet. Dr Lind (Picture 6) had discovered that fresh fruit juice was a cure for scurvy: the longer life of the middle- and upper-classes indicated that a proper diet helped people to enjoy a healthier and more prolonged life span. But until working people earned higher wages (late in the nineteenth century), such knowledge was of little use to them – they could not buy the better foods such as fruit, meat or milk.

Every country always has to make a choice as to how it will spend its annual income; if it decides to build rockets for the moon then its people can have less of something else; if the Americans spend money on a war in Vietnam they have less to spend on rebuilding their slums. In this period (1750–1830) the British people spent their annual incomes on factories, mines, canals, railways, bridges, ports and other such enterprises and these later helped the country to become even richer: but they had little left over for housing and town development in general. One of the prices paid for Britain's industrial progress is the industrial towns which still remain in Britain. They need not have been built like this – but if they had been properly built then, there would have been fewer factories and mines, and Britain's industrial progress would have been slower.

5 The Young Historian

1   Look at Picture 5 in Chapter 1 and now at Pictures 1 and 2 above. Why did the people in the houses in these pictures suffer less illness than people in Picture 3 above?

2   Look at Picture 4. Imagine you are one of the children, and write about 'Our Water Supply'.

3   Look at Picture 6 in Chapter 4. Why did the workers have to live near the factories and coal mines? Why could richer people afford to live further away from their place of work?

4   Look at Picture 3. Why were many working-class houses so dirty?

5   Draw or paint your own idea of the standpipe scene (Picture 4). This could be part of a larger frieze on industrial towns.

6   Look at Picture 7. Why is the River Thames not a sewer today?

7   Look at Picture 5. What disease was Jenner hoping to cure? Find out when innoculation became widespread as a treatment for diphtheria.

8   Dr Lind showed that scurvy could be prevented if men ate the right food. How did the work of Bakewell and other agrarian reformers help to improve the health of the British people?

6 Central and Local Government

Eighteenth-century Government

Today we expect the British government to be concerned with our schools, houses, road building, and our health; we expect to pay taxes to provide schools, hospitals, homes for old people and pensions. In the eighteenth century the British government was not concerned with any of these things; it dealt with foreign affairs – and conducted wars against Britain's enemies or made trade agreements with our friends; it dealt with colonies in America, the West Indies and India; it imposed taxes on goods entering and leaving the country so that the country's trade could be helped to grow; it passed laws so that people's property was safe from thieves and it punished wrongdoers.

The scope of its work, however, was very limited. For one thing, the national income was small and so the government could not – even had it wanted to – create a Welfare State. This had to wait until Britain was a very much richer country. For another the system of communication was very poor so that the government rarely knew what was going on in more distant parts of the country where the real government was in the hands of the Lords of the Manors or the local Justices of the Peace. Finally, the government – like the rest of the country – did not believe that it was the duty of a government to interfere in people's lives; the doctrine of *laisser-faire* – or leaving well alone – was the one which most people believed in.

Corrupt Parliament

The House of Commons (Picture 1) was one of the Houses of Parliament. Even

1   The House of Commons in 1793.

though in this picture Young Pitt is the Prime Minister addressing the Commons, the House of Lords was the more important of the two Houses. Most of the Members of the Commons were the sons of the Lords, waiting for their fathers to die so that they could go to the Lords. Many other members were elected in a corrupt election in one or other of the many constituencies in agricultural England (Picture 4). Some people thought that this system should be reformed (Picture 2) but attempts by John Wilkes, the Duke of Bedford and Pitt himself to reform Parliament failed, and after 1793 – when Britain went to war with Revolutionary France – the ruling classes came to believe that reform was the same as revolution and they opposed the former as strongly as they did the latter (Picture 3). An unreformed Parliament could not, apparently, be reformed; some people then decided that this Parliament and the whole system of government it stood for would have to be swept away. A few supported the ideas of Arthur Thistlewood who plotted at Cato Street, London, to blow up the Cabinet (Picture 7); others supported Radical reformers such as Hunt and Robert

TAKE YOUR CHOICE!

Representation and Respect:	Imposition and Contempt.

Annual Parliaments and Liberty:	Long Parliaments and Slavery.

Where annual election ends, slavery begins.
Hist. Eff. on Brit. Const.

A free government, in order to maintain itself free, hath need every day of some new provision in favour of Liberty. Machiavel.

I wish the maxim of Machiavel was followed, that of examining a constitution, at certain periods, according to its first principles; this would correct abuses and supply defects. Lord Camden.

And now—in the name of all that is holy—let us consider whether a scheme may not be laid down for obtaining the necessary reformation of parliament. Burgh.

LONDON:

Printed for J. ALMON, opposite Burlington-House, in Piccadilly.

M.DCC.LXXVI.

2 The title page of Cartwright's pamphlet advocating annual parliaments.

3 Cruikshank's cartoon on the movement for Radical Reform, 1819.

Owen, who held meetings throughout the country urging the people to demand Reform. Such a meeting at St Peter's Fields, Manchester, led to the 1819 Massacre which showed how the local Justices of the Peace and the government were determined to put down any talk of reform (Picture 8).

Local Councils

At different times in British history the rich inhabitants of growing towns had bought from the lord on whose land their town was built, the right to have their own council. By 1750 there were about 180 such towns (or boroughs) in Britain which had obtained Charters establishing their independence and allowing the setting up of borough councils. In some cases the charters named the people who would have the right to take part in such elections; in other cases the right to vote was given to all the freemen (usually the rich men) in the town.

Councils such as these were concerned mainly with making their town richer;

53

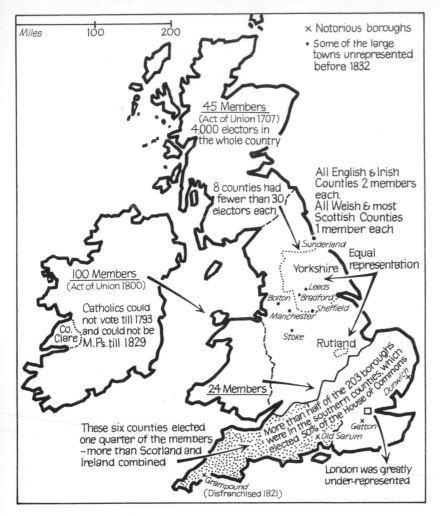

Miles 100 200

× Notorious boroughs
• Some of the large towns unrepresented before 1832

45 Members
(Act of Union 1707)
4,000 electors in the whole country

8 counties had fewer than 30 electors each

All English & Irish Counties 2 members each.
All Welsh & most Scottish Counties 1 member each

100 Members
(Act of Union 1800)

Catholics could not vote till 1793 and could not be M.Ps. till 1829

Co. Clare

Sunderland

Equal representation

Yorkshire

Leeds
Bolton Bradford
Manchester Sheffield
Stoke
Rutland

24 Members

More than half of the 203 boroughs were in the southern counties, which elected 50% of the House of Commons

Dunwich

These six counties elected one quarter of the members – more than Scotland and Ireland combined

Gatton
× Old Sarum

London was greatly under-represented

× Grampound
(Disfranchised 1821)

4 Map of the constituencies before the Reform Act of 1832.

5 'The Mock Mayor' from a painting by R. W. Buss.

they built a town market and toll gates and charged people for the use of the market or the bridge (Picture 6). Often the councillors used their position to enrich themselves. One man, for instance, would sell a field to the council for a very high price; the money would come from a tax imposed on all the towns-people – the price would be shared amongst all the councillors. Sometimes they used the local taxes to provide themselves with weekly feasts, or gifts. The townspeople often resented this corrupt system of local government, but there was little they could do about it, except make fun of it (Picture 5).

These Chartered councils had no power to deal with problems connected with the growth of their towns – housing, street cleansing, refuse disposal, etc. When it became necessary to deal with such a problem, the council or a group of the richer people would pay the money to get Parliament to pass a Private Act – applying to their town only – which allowed the people to elect another council – or Improvement Commissioners – to deal with the problem of street cleansing, refuse collection and the like. A town might then have applied for three or four Improvement Acts, each dealing with a particular problem as it became important.

6 Carlisle board showing toll charges.

Justices of the Peace

Throughout the rest of the country local government was in the hands of the Justices of the Peace. They were appointed by government to administer the laws – on poaching or murder – and to fix wages, look after the poor, see to the maintenance of law and order in general. When Britain was a country of small villages, where almost everyone knew everyone else in his village, this system worked; the local Justice, usually rich enough to have plenty of free time, would know what local problems existed and he and his colleagues would know how to deal with them. But as many large towns were built, the Justices found that they could not cope; the problems were too big for them, and they were too inexperienced to deal with them.

New towns

In these new towns – away from the Chartered Boroughs – there was no council. No method existed by which people could elect a Council until Parliament passed a Municipal Reform Act in 1835 – which is outside our period. In these new towns there was often no government at all and the town developed in its own higgledy-piggledy way; in other places there was a lord of the manor who tried to exercise some control, but he usually found that he had neither the staff nor the experience to cope with the situation. In some of the larger industrial towns – such as Manchester and Liverpool – there were enough public-spirited people (clergymen, doctors and merchants) to pay for the passing of one or more Improvement Acts which set up some form of Commissioners (or council) to deal with some of the problems of the growing town.

7   The Cato Street Conspiracy – a plan to assassinate the Cabinet, but failed.

8 The Peterloo Massacre.

In general, however, it is fair to say that little attention was paid by the central government to the problems of the industrial towns and there was, in general, insufficient power in the hands of local authorities to deal with them. Until the central government passed laws on housing and sanitation and until there were councils to see that these laws were kept, then the problems of industrial towns would continue to grow.

6 The Young Historian

1   Picture 1 shows Prime Minister Pitt addressing the House of Commons in 1793. Find out why he might have been talking about France in this debate.

2   Pitt had supported Parliamentary reform in the 1780s. Find out what he did to suggestions of reform after 1793.

3   Look again at Pictures 8 and 9 in Chapter 3 and at Picture 7 in Chapter 8. Now look at Pictures 3, 7 and 8 in this Chapter. Write a letter to a friend on the topic of 'Our violent society'.

4   Picture 2 shows the title page to a pamphlet published in 1776. Find out what (i) Cartwright, (ii) Wilkes, and (iii) Wyvill wanted as regards reform of Parliament and the electoral system.

5 Look again at Picture 9 in Chapter 1, and at Pictures 1 and 3 in Chapter 10. Who could afford to pay for libraries, schools, a proper water supply? How are these things paid for today?

6 Look at Picture 8. Read Howard Spring's *Fame is the Spur* which tells you about Peterloo.

7 Look at Picture 7. Why did many people think assassination of the Cabinet would be the only way to improve conditions in Britain?

8 Look at Picture 4, which shows the distribution of constituencies in 1830. Name six counties that had more than their fair share of MPs and six that had too few in proportion to the size of their population.

7 Poverty

Defined

As long ago as the first century AD the world was told 'The poor you have always with you'. Poverty, therefore, is no new problem, nor was it the result of the industrial revolution. There have always been families whose income has fallen, for one reason or another – so that they have not been able to obtain enough money to pay for the necessities of life. Of course there is a difference between what we in Britain today think of as poverty and what people thought a hundred years ago, because we expect people to have a higher standard of living today than would have been the case a hundred years ago. Our ideas of what is necessary for living are different to those of the people living one hundred years ago. But both then and now there have been and are people who do not have enough money to enable them to live 'properly'.

Causes

If the family's wage-earner is too sick to work or if he dies, then the family's income falls. Sickness and death were commonplace in the early industrial towns (Pictures 2 and 3), so there were many families without any regular wage-earner. When an employer is unable to sell the products of his factory he has to dismiss the workpeople. At this period (1750–1830), and for long after, there was no unemployment benefit system, so that once a workman was dismissed his income ceased, and his family had no income. Sometimes employers preferred to employ women and children rather than men (Chapter 1, Picture 6; Chapter 2, Pictures 6 and 7; Chapter 8, Pictures 4, 5, 6; and Chapter 9, Picture 7). This often meant that the men found it difficult to get work and that the wages paid to the women and children were not enough to maintain the family properly. This also meant that many families had to put up with overcrowded houses

1   The Tichborne Dole.

2 A court for King Cholera – slum conditions in the nineteenth century.

(Picture 3) and to scrabble for their food in pig troughs (Picture 6).

If the wage-earner had an accident at work so that he could not follow his employment for a time then the family income fell. Accidents were common in the iron foundries of the time (Picture 5) and in the coal mines (Chapter 8, Picture 5). Workers in cotton factories were often caught in the unfenced machinery (Chapter 8, Picture 4), resulting in severe injuries and, frequently, death. Until 1897 there was no law to force the employer to pay an injured workman any compensation and until 1911 there was no government payment of Sickness Benefit. An injured workman had no income – and his family became 'poor'.

A workman's wage might have been enough to allow him and perhaps his wife and one or two children to live properly. But when working men had large families – as many did at this time – his wage was not enough to provide food and clothing for all of them. This family then became a 'poor family', although the father was at work. There was no system of family allowances until 1945.

3 Overcrowding in a labourers cottage.

Aids to the poor

A common sight in eighteenth- and nineteenth-century Britain was the beggar; sometimes beggars were almost professionally engaged in this 'trade' as Dickens describes in *Oliver Twist*. Men injured in wars or at work, men crippled from childhood or malformed from birth, sat in the streets and waited for passers-by to drop a coin into a lap or a tin. In many places wealthier people had helped to organise some assistance for the poor; in Picture 1 you can see the distribution of aid to the poor by the the Tichborne family in the late seventeenth century. In other places church collections were used for this same purpose – to give something to poor people.

By 1601 the Tudor governments had passed laws forcing every parish to look after its own poor – by building a workhouse where work could be provided for the unemployed and shelter for the widow and orphan, the sick and the disabled. Many parishes had done so and the parish beadle (Picture 4) had as one of his many tasks the collecting of a poor rate and of looking after the poor. Dickens describes such a beadle and workhouse in *Oliver Twist*.

If food prices rise while a workman's wage remains static then he may not have enough to buy all that he needs and his family becomes poor. During the French and Napoleonic Wars there was no import of foreign food into Britain, so that the price of food rose (Chapter 3, Pictures 6 and 7). While this helped the richer farmers, it brought hardship to the working people, particularly to those who lost their income as machinery did the work they had been doing in the cottage (Chapter 1, Pictures 2 and 6; Chapter 8, Pictures 3 and 4). Even

4 The Parish Beadle was responsible for running the Poor House.

those who had work found wage rates very low since the employers could choose from among many working people and could afford to offer only low wages.

One method of coping with the problem of low wages was devised by the Justices of the Peace at Speenhamland, near Newbury in Berkshire:

> ... the Magistrates now present have unanimously resolved that they will ... make the following calculations and allowances for relief of all ... industrious men and their families who, to the satisfaction of the Justices of their Parish, shall endeavour (as far as they can) for their own support and maintenance. That is to say, when the loaf of flour, weighing 8 lb. 11 oz. shall cost 1s.
>
> Then every poor and industrious man shall have for his support 3s. weekly, either produced by his own or his family's labour, or an allowance from the poor rates; and for the support of his wife and every other of his family, 1s. 6d.
>
> When the loaf shall cost 1s. 4d.
>
> Then every poor and industrious man shall have 4s. weekly for his own, and 1s. 10d. for the support of every other of his family.
>
> And ... as the price of bread rises or falls ... 3d. to the man, and 1d. to every other of the family on every 1d. by which the loaf rise above 1s.

(*Reading Mercury*, 11 May, 1795).

6 Ragged children round a trough.

Since each parish was supposed to look after its own poor, the government passed laws against 'wandering beggars' who might have been born in one parish but, in the course of wandering around England, might become a burden on another parish. Acts of Settlement compelled people to return to their own parish if they wanted relief.

Opposition to Poor Law

Some people were opposed to helping the poor because they were afraid that this would keep alive people who could marry and have children and so increase the number of poor people. Other people argued that keeping the poor alive meant that the nation's income had to be divided among more mouths than would be the case if they were left to die. Since this meant a smaller share in the income for everyone they argued that this was unfair to those who were working. If the poor were left to die there would be more for everyone.

Another group of people argued that the cost of looking after the poor was growing all the time – either because the cost of food was going up or because there were increasing numbers of poor people. Such people argued that this could not be allowed to continue; they wanted a tidying-up process to take place so that only the really poor were helped.

63

7 A cartoon on the agricultural labourers' riots in the 1830s.

8 The Bristol Reform riots in Queen's Square, October 1831.

Reform

However, such proposals were not accepted by 1830. It was not until a Whig Government was elected in 1830 that a Commission was set up to look into the workings of the Poor Law. Their proposals and the subsequent changes in Poor Law took place outside our period.

7 The Young Historian

1 Look at Picture 2 and look again at Pictures 4 and 7 in Chapter 5. Why did many fathers die in the early industrial towns? What happened to their families?

2 Look at Picture 1. This is an example of charity being given to poor people in the late seventeenth century. Why is there less need for this sort of charity for (i) old people, (ii) sick people than there used to be?

3 Look at Picture 4. Find out the name of the novel which Charles Dickens wrote in which such a beadle was an important character.

4 Look at Picture 5. Can you say why there were many accidents in such foundries and in mines (Chapter 2, Pictures 4 and 7) and mills (Chapter 2, Picture 6)?

5 Find out when employers were first forced to pay compensation to workmen who had been injured at work. What do you think happened to the workman and his family before that time?

6 Look at Picture 6. Imagine that you are one of the children and explain to your country cousin (Chapter 1, Pictures 2 and 4) why you are behaving like this.

7 Look at Picture 7 and look again at Chapter 3, Pictures 8 and 9. Why did so many of the workers riot?

8 Draw or paint (perhaps as part of a large frieze) your own 'Poor people in the early nineteenth-century towns'.

8 Trade Unions and Working Conditions

Gilds

In medieval England each craft had its gild – a society to which all the craftsmen belonged and to which they paid a weekly subscription, in return for a pension when too old to work, or some money when sick. The gild had a president and other officials, one of whom was the warden. His job concerned the apprentices who had to learn the trade from a craftsmen. After six or seven years of apprenticeship a young man would bring some of his work to the warden and if it was good enough the apprentice would get a certificate showing that he was now a qualified worker. He then went to work as a day labourer or as a journeyman for one of the master craftsmen until he had saved enough money to buy all the tools of his trade: then he, too, could set up as a master craftsman. So every apprentice had the chance to become a master – and an employer.

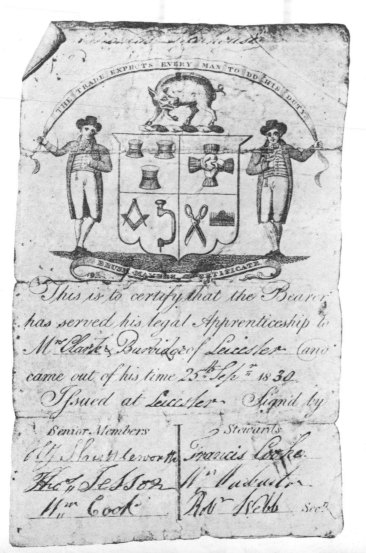

1 An early Trade union membership card.

Workers' gilds

But by 1750 this was no longer the case. There were some trades where the cost of setting up in business was too high. Very few miners or iron workers, for instance, would be able to set up on their own. There were other trades where the masters refused to allow new masters to set up – the masters' gilds had become selfish. This meant that most apprentices knew they could never become employers and would always remain paid labourers. Not surprisingly these journeymen soon learned to group together – in journeymen gilds – as their masters had done in craft gilds. These journeymen gilds tried to force the masters to negotiate on wages and hours, and did the work that today is done by a trade union.

Wage-fixing

In Tudor times the government had said that the Justices of the Peace were to fix wage rates for farm labourers and other workers. At first this seemed fair to the workers, who had no unions; but by 1750 many journeymen gilds wanted freedom to bargain with their employers and did not want the Justices involved in the business of wage-fixing. Very often the Justices were related to employers; almost always they belonged to the same social class as the employer so that their decisions appeared to favour the employer and not the worker. But when the gilds tried to force the eighteenth-century employer to deal with them the employer appealed to the law (which said that Justices were to fix wages) and got the Parliament to pass Acts which forbade the gilds to deal with wages and hours of work.

Eighteenth-century anti-union laws

This did not stop the Durham miners or the London weavers, and other local groups of workers, from forming their gilds. And as the nature of industry changed from the domestic to the factory system, so that there were even more workers

2 Enrolling in a trade union.

and fewer chances of a worker becoming an employer, the number of such gilds grew. By the end of the eighteenth century the British government led by William Pitt was involved in a war against the French. This war had put an end to Pitt's ideas of reforming the corrupt Parliament (Chapter 6); it also made many of the English ruling class fear any ideas of change or reform (Chapter 6, Pictures 2 and 3): they were afraid that the English working class might follow the French example and start a revolution in England (Chapter 6, Pictures 7 and 8). In 1799 the government accepted the advice of William Wilberforce, MP, and passed the first Combination Act. This, and later Combination Acts, made it illegal for men to form unions, or gilds, for the purpose of negotiating about wages or conditions of work. They could still form a society of workers to provide pensions, sick pay and another benefits for each other, but such societies could not deal with wages or conditions of work.

Repeal of Combination Acts

By 1824 the French wars had been over for nearly ten years; trade had recovered and Britain was once again prosperous. A new government with Huskisson, Peel and Canning, was passing a number of reforms through Parliament. Francis Place, a former union member, but now an employer as a Charing Cross tailor, and Joseph Hume a reforming MP, managed to persuade William Huskisson (President of the Board of Trade), that the Combination Acts should be abolished. In 1824 they were repealed so that unions could be formed to deal with the

3   Working in the home.

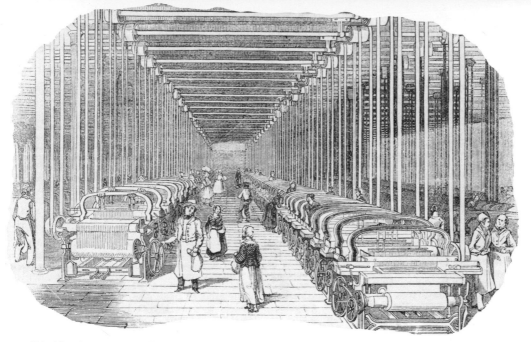

4 Working in a cotton mill.

problems of wages and conditions. Hundreds of unions were formed – until railways were built most of them were made up of workers in one locality only. But the employers still opposed the setting up of unions. They sacked any man suspected of belonging to a union; many of them made their employees sign a document, such as this one from Derby:

> We the undersigned do declare that we are not in any way connected with the General Union and that we do not and will not contribute to the support of such members as may be out of work in consequence of belonging to such Union. June 15th 1833.

Workers who refused to sign were sacked.

When, in spite of this, unions were formed, many employers simply closed their factories and locked the men out until they had agreed to give up their membership and come back to work on the employers' terms.

Even though the law allowed unions to be formed there were many examples of employers using other laws as an excuse for persecution of union members. The most famous example was the case of the Tolpuddle weavers (Picture 7) who were arrested for having formed a union but were tried on the excuse that they had broken a law which forbade the taking of secret oaths (Picture 2).

Early factories

With the employers and the Justices still opposed to trade unions it is not surprising that by 1830 (the end of our present study) the majority of the poorly-paid and often ignorant workers did not belong to any union. These people were the first and second generation of workers in the industrial towns. They had either worked in, or had heard about, the domestic system (Chapter 1, Picture 2;

and Picture 3 here), where the hours of work were fixed by the mother or father and where the family wage was paid when they sold their yarn or cloth. But in the factory (Picture 4) or mine (Picture 5), the men, women and children worked under the rule of an employer who fixed the hours of work and decided what wages he would offer. Since there were plenty of people ready to work for him, the employer could make the people work long hours (from before sunrise until after sunset) for very low wages: three shillings per week for a child, and six or seven shillings for an adult. Some children suffered a great deal from harsh employers, as can be seen from this extract from the evidence presented to the Select Committee on Factory Children's Labour (1831–32):

Evidence of Samuel Coulson

Q. At what time in the morning, in the brisk time, did those girls go to the mills?

A. In the brisk time, for about six weeks, they have gone at 3 o'clock in the morning, and ended at 10, or nearly half-past at night.

Q. What intervals were allowed for rest or refreshment during those nineteen hours of labour?

6 Children in the brick yards.

A. Breakfast a quarter of an hour, and dinner half an hour, and drinking a quarter of an hour.

Q. Was any of that time taken up in cleaning the machinery?

A. They generally had to do what they call dry down; sometimes this took the whole of the time at breakfast or drinking, and they were to get their dinner or breakfast as they could; if not, it was brought home.

Not all employers were bad; many, especially those who had large factories and made large profits, tried to make working conditions as good as possible. The factories were clean, and though the hours of work were kept to about twelve per day, the children were treated kindly. But many, especially those who owned small factories and were trying to make enough profit to set themselves up in larger factories, were less kind. Conditions in their factories were

7 On the day after this notice was issued the Tolpuddle weavers were arrested.

CAUTION.

WHEREAS it has been represented to us from several quarters, that mischievous and designing Persons have been for some time past, endeavouring to induce, and have induced, many Labourers in various Parishes in this County, to attend Meetings, and to enter into Illegal Societies or Unions, to which they bind themselves by unlawful oaths, administered secretly by Persons concealed, who artfully deceive the ignorant and unwary,—WE, the undersigned Justices think it our duty to give this PUBLIC NOTICE and CAUTION, that all Persons may know the danger they incur by entering into such Societies.

ANY PERSON who shall become a Member of such a Society, or take any Oath, or assent to any Test or Declaration not authorized by Law—

Any Person who shall administer, or be present at, or consenting to the administering or taking any Unlawful Oath, or who shall cause such Oath to be administered, although not actually present at the time—

Any Person who shall not reveal or discover any Illegal Oath which may have been administered, or any Illegal Act done or to be done—

Any Person who shall induce, or endeavour to persuade any other Person to become a Member of such Societies,

WILL BECOME

Guilty of Felony,

AND BE LIABLE TO BE

Transported for Seven Years.

ANY PERSON who shall be compelled to take such an Oath, unless he shall declare the same within four days, together with the whole of what he shall know touching the same, will be liable to the same Penalty.

Any Person who shall directly or indirectly maintain correspondence or intercourse with such Society, will be deemed Guilty of an Unlawful Combination and Confederacy, and on Conviction before one Justice, on the Oath of one Witness, be liable to a Penalty of TWENTY POUNDS, or to be committed to the Common Gaol or House of Correction, for THREE CALENDAR MONTHS; or if proceeded against by Indictment, may be CONVICTED OF FELONY, and be TRANSPORTED FOR SEVEN YEARS.

Any Person who shall knowingly permit any Meeting of any such Society to be held in any House, Building, or other Place, shall for the first offence be liable to the Penalty of FIVE POUNDS; and for every other offence committed after Conviction, be deemed Guilty of such Unlawful Combination and Confederacy, and on Conviction before one Justice, on the Oath of one Witness, be liable to a Penalty of TWENTY POUNDS, or to Commitment to the Common Gaol or House of Correction, FOR THREE CALENDAR MONTHS; or if proceeded against by Indictment may be

CONVICTED OF FELONY,
And Transported for SEVEN YEARS.

COUNTY OF DORSET,   C. B. WOLLASTON,   HENRY FRAMPTON,
Dorchester Division.   JAMES FRAMPTON,   RICHD. TUCKER STEWARD,
     WILLIAM ENGLAND,   WILLIAM R. CHURCHILL,
February 22d. 1834.   THOS. DADE,   AUGUSTUS FOSTER.
     JNO. MORTON COLSON.

G. CLARK, PRINTER, CORNHILL, DORCHESTER.

very harsh and their treatment of children very cruel. At first Parliament tried to pass laws so that orphan children sent by the Poor Law authorities to work in the mills would get some protection; Parliament felt that men and women, and children with parents, could look after themselves. But even these Acts (1802 and 1819) never really worked because Parliament did not appoint independent Inspectors to go around the factories to make sure that employers obeyed the law. This was left to the local Justices of the Peace – and they were unwilling to take sides against the employers.

There was no effective Factory Act passed by 1830, so that people continued to work in dirty, dangerous mills and mines and children continued to do heavy and dirty work, such as carrying clay in the brickfields (Picture 6). The national income was growing rapidly during this whole period 1750–1830. One of the reasons for its growth was that the workers were getting only a small share of this income so that more of it could be used to build bigger factories and mines; more efficient machines and railways. They had to wait for another period – until they formed their unions and until governments passed laws about working conditions – before sharing in the nation's prosperity.

8 The Young Historian

1   Look at Picture 1. What is the trade of this union member? Why did such craftsmen try to limit the number of people joining their craft?

2   Picture 2 is an artist's impression of the enrolling of a new union member in the early nineteenth century. What sort of oath is the new member taking?

3   Look at Picture 3. Why did these workers not need a Trade Union as much as did workers in the industrial mills and mines?

4   Picture 4 shows the interior of a mill. Why was it easier for workers in such mills to form trade unions than it had been for the domestic workers?

5   Look at Picture 5. If you were one of these workers what sort of things would you want your union to concern itself with?

6   Picture 6 shows a child working in a brickyard where they carried very heavy weights for very long hours. Why did their parents allow them to do this work?

7   Picture 7 shows the notice put up in Tolpuddle in 1834. Find out when (i) Trade Unions were legalised and men allowed to form them, (ii) what happened to the men at Tolpuddle who tried to form a union.

8   By 1830 (the end of the period covered by this book) several politicians had tried to get laws passed to stop the employment of children in cotton mills. Find out something about these attempts and show why they were not successful.

9 Women and the Family

One of the biggest changes that has taken place in the last thirty years (1940–1970) has been in the place of women in our society. Today women have equal rights with men – they can vote, work, keep their property if they have any, obtain a divorce, go to university or college – in fact they can do most things which a free man can do. Most of these changes have taken place in the recent past – nearly all of them in the twentieth century.

Eighteenth-century ladies

In 1750 women were regarded as inferior to men in every way. In the villages and small towns of England the aristocratic and middle-class woman (Picture 1) was expected to be the outward sign of her husband's success; she dressed, rode in a carriage and commanded servants – all of which her husband had provided for her and all of which he could take away from her. Her daughters were supposed to find husbands for themselves so that they too would become 'beautiful birds in a gilded cage', and mothers arranged huge balls (Picture 2) so that their daughters might meet the right young men.

1   A prosperous family drinking tea – a new fashion in the eighteenth century.

2   Ball in Cyfarthfa Castle.

3   A middle class family.

4   The Royal Crescent, Bath.

5   A Dame School.

With the industrial changes of the period (1750–1830), the number of rich industrialists and bankers grew and so did the number of the middling rich – engineers, contractors, lawyers, architects and so on. For their families life was comfortable; the sons went to one of the old or new public schools (Chapter 10, Picture 1) or to one of the old grammar schools (Chapter 10, Picture 3). After this the son began his career and in time became the head of a family. The daughters of these rich families might be taught at home by a governess (Chapter 10, Picture 2) while they learned the female arts of sewing, running a home, music and singing.

Eighteenth-century Working women

The women of the lower classes had always worked – either in the cottage (Chapter 1, Picture 2) or in industry (Chapter 1, Picture 1). When they moved into the factory towns they continued to work – in mine or mill – and so did their children. Some middle-class women might have wanted the freedom to go to work – the working-class women would have welcomed the freedom to stay at home away from work. But they had to work because their families needed their wages.

Large families

Women of both upper and lower classes had large families in this and later periods. Sometimes a number of their children died at birth or soon afterwards;

6 Family group painted by F. Wheatley.

7 Child labour in the mines.

we know that about half the children in Manchester died before they were five, and that similar figures exist for Liverpool, Leeds, and other towns. However, the large family, of five or more children, was common in England at this time. This helps to explain the poverty of many families – the wages took no account of the size of the family, nor was there any system of family allowances such as we have today.

The size of the family also helps to explain why women had such a poor position in society. A woman's task was to bring up her children. Married at twenty-five (or later) she spent the next ten years in childbearing and was about forty before the youngest of her children reached the age of five or thereabouts. By then she was physically worn out after a very hard life. Even as late as 1850 the average expectation of life for women was only forty-two. Was it worth providing women with education, job-training and so on if there was little or no chance of their using this training?

Many of the mothers died in childbirth, leaving the older children to fend for themselves. This is one of the reasons for the many child beggars found in the streets of London and other industrial towns. Other orphan children were looked after by the Poor Law and were sent to work in the mills and mines; others just ran wild, as Dickens describes in *Oliver Twist*, where Fagin has taken charge of a gang of such children.

8 Child beggar from Cruikshank's engraving 'The Bottle'.

9 The Young Historian

1   What differences would a child notice between life in Cyfarthfa Castle (Picture 2) and Birmingham (Chapter 1, Picture 8)?

2   Paint or draw (perhaps as part of a large frieze) your own (i) lady in a gown (Picture 2) or (ii) child beggar (Picture 8).

3   Look at Picture 3. The number of such families increased between 1750 and 1830. Why? Find out (i) the names of three schools to which they sent their sons, and (ii) three holiday resorts visited by such families.

4   Why did rich people go to Bath (Picture 4)? Draw or paint this scene.

5   Why did the children in Picture 7 rarely, if ever, go to school? Do you envy them?

6   Write a letter as written by one of the children in Picture 6 who has just seen children at work (Picture 7). Find out the name of the rich lord who was so horrified by seeing children working that he became their champion and forced Parliament to pass many laws to prevent the employment of children.

7   Look at Picture 5. Why were schools like this called Dame Schools? Can you say why many children learned very little at such schools?

8   What was the occupation of the man who owned Cyfarthfa Castle (Picture 2)? How were families such as these made richer by the building of railways (Chapter 4, Picture 7).

10 Education

In 1750 England was a much poorer country than it is today. Most people were employed in farming where, because of the strip system (Chapter 3, Picture 5) and the poor tools (Chapter 1, Picture 3), their income was low. There was a certain amount of industry but, even here, the mines and factories were small (Chapter 1, Picture 1) and the output low. Since the country was not very rich (as it is today) there was less money to spare for such luxuries as education.

Public Schools

There was also little need for education for most people. The cottage worker, using hand-driven machinery (Chapter 1, Picture 2), did not require much training; nor did the industrial worker in the copper and other industries (Chapter 1, Picture 1). The country had to be governed – by MPs, Justices of the Peace, and Civil Servants – and the army and navy had to have competent, trained officers; for those sons of the aristocracy there were the boarding schools such as Eton, Harrow, Winchester, and so on. You can read about life in these schools in the opening chapters of the lives of politicians such as Gladstone or Lord Melbourne; you may already have read the famous novel *Tom Brown's Schooldays* which tells of the reforms of these schools by Dr Arnold of Rugby (Picture 1).

1   The Southern Schools and Dormitories of Rugby School.

The rich man's daughters rarely, if ever, left home for school. They were taught at home by governesses such as the one in Picture 2, or as described in the opening chapters of William Thackeray's *Vanity Fair*. Some wealthy children went to the local grammar school if one existed.

Grammar Schools

In many parts of the country – and particularly in the agricultural south – there were a number of grammar schools. These had been founded in the fifteenth and sixteenth centuries – sometimes by the monarch (hence the various King Edward VI schools in the Midlands and elsewhere, and the Queen Elizabeth schools in several parts of the country). Other people had followed their monarch's example and had left money in their wills for the local mayor or borough council (Chapter 6) to start schools where the sons (and sometimes the daughters) of the shop-keepers, tradesmen, skilled workers and better-off farmers might learn Latin, Greek and Ancient History, as well as their religion.

Some people wanted their children to be taught science and mathematics, to fit them for the increasingly scientific world. In 1777 the governors of the Leeds Grammar School tried to force the headmaster to introduce these subjects;

2   The family governess.

3 Plymouth Grammar School.

he refused and, after a series of court cases, the Lord Chancellor decided in 1805:

> that he could not allow the conversion of that Institution by filling a school intended for that mode of Education with scholars studying the German and French languages, Mathematics, and anything save Greek and Latin. This is a scheme to promote the benefits of the Merchants of Leeds. It is not that the poor inhabitants are to be taught reading and writing English, but the Clerks and Riders of the Merchants are to be taught French and German to carry on a trade. I fear the effect would be to turn out the poor Latin and Greek scholars altogether.

Private Schools

Most of these grammar schools were very small – taking in perhaps forty or fifty children. In many parts of the country there were no such schools. To make

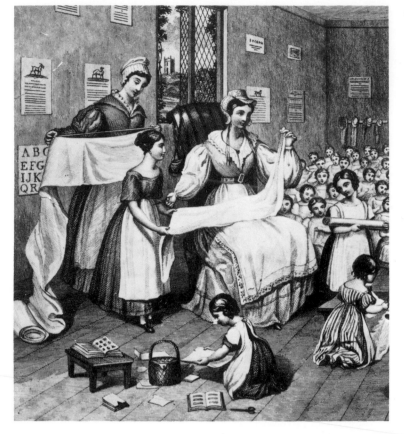

up for this lack of schools for the better-off townspeople, private schools had been started. In some cases the owner of the private school was a university graduate and his pupils would be taught well; very often the owner was unqualified and children learned very little. Private schools such as these are described in the opening chapters of Dickens' *Great Expectations*, although his most famous example of such a school was Dotheboys Hall to which Nicholas Nickelby went.

Dame Schools

For those who could not afford the fees for the boarding or grammar school, nor the private day school, there was the Dame School where a vicar's daughter, or a widow of a tradesman, took in a dozen or so children, teaching them in her home for 2d or 3d a week. She had no training, very often little learning, and could teach little.

Charity Schools

In the seventeenth-century the Anglican Church had tried to start a working-class school in every parish. Wealthier members of the Church were asked to contribute to a school fund out of which a schoolroom could be built. An annual collection was taken to pay for the teacher and equipment, and parents were invited to pay a small fee (2d a week) if they could afford it. By 1750 these schools had become known as Charity Schools and under the influence of very active people some of these schools were in good condition – the buildings were good, the teachers were keen and the children attended in large numbers. Hannah More was very active in founding many of these Charity Schools, and she wrote:

> My plan of instruction is extremely simple and limited. They learn on weekdays such coarse work as may fit them for servants. I allow of no writing for the poor. My object is not to make fanatics, but to train up the lower classes in habits of industry and piety . . .

Many parents could not afford to allow their children to go to any school at all; they needed the children to work at home (Chapter 1, Picture 2); others were ashamed to let their children go because of the lack of clothing. One clergyman, giving evidence to a Parliamentary Committee on the Education of the Lower Orders in the Metropolis and Beyond (1816) reported:

> We found that there were a great many who did not go to any school; the reason assigned in some measure for it was their ragged condition, and their being unfit, from their great poverty, to appear decently at any school. . . . But there are a great many mendicants in our parish, owing to the extreme lowness of some part of the neighbourhood, and the more children they have, the more success they meet with in begging, and they keep them in that way; so that in the weekday we could not get them to a day school without some different measures were adopted; neither are they fit to appear in them as they are; and on a Sunday they get more by begging than they do on any other day in the week, because more people are out and about; we tried the experiment in several instances, by giving clothes to some of the most ragged, in order to bring them decent to school; they appeared for one Sunday or two, and then disappeared and the clothes disappeared also . . .

The Methodist Church started Sunday Schools for such working children (and their parents) and the idea of such schools was taken up by Robert Raikes of Gloucester, who worked hard to persuade other Churches in many towns to follow the Methodists' example.

Monitorial Schools
By 1800 the population of many towns had grown as factories were built, and workers came to live nearby. Now there were a number of towns with populations between 50,000 and 100,000. In such towns there were a large number of children – too many for the Sunday schools and Charity schools to cope with even if

5 A monitorial school.

such schools existed there. Two men – an Anglican vicar, Andrew Bell, and a Quaker, Joseph Lancaster – working in different parts of the country at about the same time, hit on the same idea of educating large numbers of poor children. If rich people would provide the money for a large hall (or schoolroom) in which 500 or more children could sit on benches (Picture 5) then one teacher, with the help of a few older pupils, could teach 500 or 700 children. This 'monitorial' method seemed to work; the teacher gave a lesson to a small group of older boys (or monitors) who then went around the hall giving the same lesson to a group of children at their benches. King George III was the most notable contributor to Lancaster's work – but rich people everywhere were persuaded to give large sums of money so that such schools could be built and poor children educated – often for nothing.

You will notice that the government had nothing to do with any of these different kinds of schools. Some MPs tried after 1800 to get Parliament to pass laws which would force the government either to start their own schools or to give money to the schools started by Lancaster and Bell. But neither the government, nor most MPs, believed that this was something they should do.

During the period 1750–1830 the country became richer as industry spread and output increased. Some of this increased wealth was used to build more factories and machines, some of it was used to build new houses for richer people and crowded houses for the workers. But the government did not believe that it had the right to take any part of this increased wealth for use in education – or for helping the old (Chapter 7) or the sick (Chapter 5). This was the period when people were free from government control over their lives and their money.

6 A Dame school.

7 Girl at play with a shuttlecock.

10 The Young Historian

1   You would enjoy reading *Tom Brown's Schooldays* by Thomas Hughes. It is a story about life at Rugby school (Picture 1).

2   Why were public schools and grammar schools mainly for boys?

3   Write a letter as written by a girl being taught by the governess. Why did rich families allow governesses to teach their girls?

4   Imagine that you were a child at the Dame School. Write an account of a day there, and paint or draw it.

5   Many grammar schools (Picture 3) were built in the sixteenth century. Find out if there is such a school in your district. What sort of children went to (i) boarding schools such as Rugby (Picture 1) and (ii) grammar schools.

6   Look at Picture 5. Why could one person not teach all the children in this schoolroom? Why were such schools called 'Monitorial' schools?

7   Find out when the government first gave a grant to help educate more people. To whom was this grant given?

8   All the schools shown in this chapter were paid for by private subscription. Who pays for most of the schools in your town today? Why are more schools needed in modern Britain than were needed in Britain in the eighteenth century?

11 Entertainment

Mid-Eighteenth Century

Today we are used to the idea of people going abroad for a holiday; we have television and record players in the home, cinema and theatre in our towns, newspapers and libraries – a dozen different ways of being entertained or of entertaining ourselves. In the eighteenth century people had to find their own entertainment in their own village or town. The very rich entertained each each other in their homes, and the rich industrialists soon learned to imitate them (Chapter 9, Picture 2). The rich also hunted and shot (Picture 2) and they shared this sport with the small farmer. There were inter-village cricket matches (Picture 1) in which the landowning classes mixed freely with the ordinary people.

1 An eighteenth century cricket match.

88   **2** The Hunt – a painting by G. Morland.

There was also a mixing of the classes in the celebrations which surrounded the Christian festivals. Samuel Bamford, recalling his childhood in the late eighteenth century, wrote:

> ... the Christmas holidays always commenced on the first Monday after New Year's Day ... the sexton of the church and the ringers went from house to house wishing their neighbours 'a merry Christmas', when they were generally invited to sit down, and were presented with a jug of ale and a present in money. This was done at most of the houses ...

He recalls a holiday on Shrove Tuesday, when: 'We went to each other's houses to turn our pancakes', and mid-Lent Sunday when: 'it was customary to eat cymbeline cake and drink mulled ale ...'

He also writes:

> Easter was a more important holiday time. On Good Friday children took little baskets neatly trimmed with moss, and went a 'peace-egging', and received at some places eggs, at some places spiced loaf, and at others half-pennies. On Easter Monday, companies of young men grotesquely dressed, led up by a fiddler, and with one or two in female attire, would go from house to house on the same errand of 'peace-egging'. Meantime, the holiday having fairly commenced, all work was abandoned, good eating, good drinking, and new clothing were the order of the day. Men thronged to the ale-houses and there was much folly, intemperance and quarrelling amidst the prevailing good humour.

The Church's year provided one common link between people of all classes; another link was provided by the seasons of the year; the whole village joined in such things as haymaking, potato-picking and the like, while Harvest Festival was a celebration in which both nature and the Church joined together.

Town life

The middle-class merchants and industrialists often formed clubs of one sort or another; there were literary and debating societies for one group, amateur theatrical societies for another, and gambling clubs for a third group. The working classes with little money to spend on entertainment were unable to afford these luxuries until later in the nineteenth century. Their entertainment was often very cruel. They enjoyed the bloodletting and gambling at cock fights (Picture 3) and the brutality of rat-fighting (Picture 4).

They had no television or wireless and could not afford to pay for tickets for the theatre (Picture 8); there was free entertainment anyway from such spectacles as the public execution (Picture 5) – the last of which took place in 1849. Both rich and poor shared a common interest in gambling (Picture 6).

The Prince Regent had made Brighton a popular resort for very rich people

3 Cock fighting.

4 Rat catching – the celebrated dog Billy killing 100 rats at the Westminster Pitt, 1827.

5 A public execution at Newgate Prison, 1809.

and elsewhere in the country the rich escaped from the industrial and commercial towns for a visit to the seaside (Picture 7), but until the railways had provided a cheap method of travel this was impossible for the less wealthy.

National income and leisure

A poor country can provide only a very limited quantity and quality of entertainment for its people. It cannot afford to build many theatres or halls, it cannot free people from agriculture or industry to become actors or musicians. As England became richer during this period (1750–1830) there was more money for such things; Brighton (Picture 7) and Scarborough were developed as resorts; new theatres and clubs were built in the expanding towns. But for ordinary people there was still insufficient money to share in the leisure pursuits of their betters. They had to wait until the country had become even richer before they too could enjoy a night at the music hall or theatre. Their working life was hard (Chapter 8); their living conditions were poor (Chapter 7); it is not surprising that their ways of spending their free time were often quite brutal.

6 Gambling at St James's.

7 Seaside bathing at Brighton.

8 Drury Lane Theatre.

11 The Young Historian

1 Picture 1 shows a cricket match. Why were such matches usually played only between neighbouring villages? Find out when the present Cricket Championship system began.

2 Picture 2 shows a hunting scene. Why could country people and not townspeople enjoy this sport? Do you think that the labourer (Chapter 1, Picture 4) joined in?

3 Picture 5 shows a public execution. Do you think that the spectators have come to show grief or to enjoy themselves? Find out when the last public execution was held in Britain.

4 What kind of people could afford to go to the seaside (Picture 7)? The railway system was not built until after 1830. How did people get to the seaside before this?

5 Can you pick out three examples of brutal sports in these pictures? Find out when they were made illegal.

6 Why was there more chance of finding a theatre (Picture 8) in Birmingham (Chapter 1, Picture 8) than in a village?

7 Draw or paint your own idea of either (i) the cricket match or (ii) the theatre.

8 Why did people in the early industrial towns (Chapter 1, Pictures 6 and 8; Chapter 2, Pictures 6 and 7; Chapter 5, Pictures 3 and 4; Chapter 7, Pictures 2, 3, 4 and 5) have little time or money to spend on leisure pursuits?

James Watt, 1736–1819.
(Detail)

Charles, Viscount Townshend,
1674–1738 *(Detail)*

Thomas Telford, 1757–1834
(Detail)

John Wilkes, 1727–1797.
(Detail)

Robert Raikes, 1735–1811.
(Detail)

Jane Austen, 1775–1817.
(Detail)

Mary Wollstonecraft
Godwin, 1759–1797. *(Detail)*

Robert Owen, 1771–1858.
(Detail)

William Pitt, the Elder,
1708–1778. *(Detail)*

John Wesley, 1703–1791
(Detail)

T. H. Malthus,
(Detail)

Jeremy Bentham, 1748–1832.
(Detail)

Index

Numbers in **bold** type refer to pages on which illustrations appear.

95